Our Greatest Weapon Is Love

Our Greatest Weapon Is Love

The Essential Writings of Christophe Munzihirwa, SJ

CHRISTOPHE MUNZIHIRWA

Edited and translated by
JOHN KIESS

CASCADE *Books* · Eugene, Oregon

OUR GREATEST WEAPON IS LOVE
The Essential Writings of Christophe Munzihirwa, SJ

Copyright © 2024 Wipf and Stock Publishers. All rights reserved. Except for brief quotations in critical publications or reviews, no part of this book may be reproduced in any manner without prior written permission from the publisher. Write: Permissions, Wipf and Stock Publishers, 199 W. 8th Ave., Suite 3, Eugene, OR 97401.

Cascade Books
An Imprint of Wipf and Stock Publishers
199 W. 8th Ave., Suite 3
Eugene, OR 97401

www.wipfandstock.com

PAPERBACK ISBN: 978-1-7252-5805-1
HARDCOVER ISBN: 978-1-7252-5806-8
EBOOK ISBN: 978-1-7252-5807-5

Cataloguing-in-Publication data:

Names: Munzihirwa, Christophe, author. | Kiess, John, editor and translator.

Title: Our greatest weapon is love : the essential writings of Christophe Munzihirwa, SJ / Christophe Munzihirwa ; edited and translated by John Kiess.

Description: Eugene, OR : Cascade Books, 2024 | Includes bibliographical references and index.

Identifiers: ISBN 978-1-7252-5805-1 (paperback) | ISBN 978-1-7252-5806-8 (hardcover) | ISBN 978-1-7252-5807-5 (ebook)

Subjects: LCSH: Catholic Church—Congo (Democratic Republic)—Clergy. | Pastoral theology—Congo (Democratic Republic). | Christianity and culture—Congo (Democratic Republic). | Christian ethics—Africa. | Christian ethics—Catholic authors. | Africa.

Classification: BJ980 .M86 2024 (paperback) | BJ980 .M86 (ebook)

06/26/24

Unless otherwise noted, Scripture quotations are taken from the New Revised Standard Version Updated Edition. Copyright © 2021 National Council of Churches of Christ in the United States of America. Used by permission. All rights reserved worldwide.

Munzihirwa, Christophe. "Pour un chrétien, quelle développement?" *Zaïre-Afrique* 197 (1985) 403–11.

———. "Nation en voie de création ou pays en développement? Pour promouvoir la nation Zaïroise." *Zaïre-Afrique* 219 (1987) 519–28.

———. "Traditions culturelles et développement socio-économique." *Zaïre-Afrique* 240 (1989) 533–39.

———. "Democratie: Laquelle? Pour quoi?" *Zaïre-Afrique* 248 (1990) 349–59.

———. "La grande palabra que nous appelons conférence nationale." *Zaïre-Afrique* 257 (1991) 343–47.

*For the people of Bukavu,
who keep Munzihirwa's memory and legacy alive*

Contents

Acknowledgments | xi
Introduction | 1

PART I | DEVELOPMENT, DEMOCRACY, AND CITIZENSHIP

For a Christian, What Is Development? (1985) | 31

Building a Nation or Developing a Country? Towards the Promotion of the Zairian Nation (1987) | 43

Cultural Traditions and Socio-Economic Development (1989) | 55

Democracy: What Kind? What For? (1990) | 63

The Great Palaver We Call the National Conference (1991) | 75

PART II | THE CHRISTIAN LIFE

Meditation on the Anniversary of My Ordination (August 17, 1983) | 83

Paschal Meditation (Undated) | 85

The Cry of the Poor: On the Occasion of Lent (February 28, 1994) | 92

"With the Family, Everything Will Be Reborn": On the Year of the Family (1994) | 95

Homily from Installation as Archbishop of Bukavu (June 26, 1994) | 100

Christmas: A Challenge to Human Plans (1994) | 104

New Year Pastoral Letter (1995) | 108

On Silence (May 1995) | 112

CONTENTS

PART III | THE RWANDAN REFUGEE CRISIS

Homily from the Mass for Refugees and the Peace of All (July 24, 1994) | 117

May the Peace of Christ Dwell among Us (July 31, 1994) | 119

Letter to UN Secretary General Boutros Boutros-Ghali (August 2, 1994) | 121

Do the Nations Want to Serve the Great Lakes Region of Africa? The Church Faces the Challenge of Violence and Hypocrisy (August 3, 1994) | 122

Letter of Protest (August 23, 1994) | 128

S.O.S. from the Archbishop of Bukavu on Behalf of the Refugees (September 8, 1994) | 130

Insecurity in Bukavu (September 8, 1994) | 132

Letter to Misereor Representative (September 19, 1994) | 135

Homily from Mass at Saio Military Camp (October 15, 1994) | 138

Letter to Cardinal Danneels (President, Pax Christi) and Monsignor Delaporte (Justice and Peace, France) (January 16, 1995) | 142

The Social Situation in Bukavu Today (April 28, 1995) | 144

Letter to the Christian Consortium for Central Africa (April 28, 1995) | 146

Second Letter to UN Secretary General Boutros Boutros-Ghali (May 15, 1995) | 148

Concerning the Forced Repatriation of the Rwandan Refugees (August 24, 1995) | 151

Letter to the High Commissioner for Refugees (October 6, 1995) | 154

Letter to the Chief of Staff of the Zairian Armed Forces (FAZ), Major General Eluki Monga Aundu (November 6, 1995) | 156

Memorandum to Admiral Mavua Mudima, Vice-Minister of Defense (November 10, 1995) | 158

Forty-Three Days before Christmas (November 12, 1995) | 160

Letter to the Refugees (November 18, 1995) | 161

Christmas Letter (1995) | 163

CONTENTS

Letter to President Jimmy Carter (January 30, 1996) | 168
Letter to the Church (April 12, 1996) | 171
Letter to the American Ambassador (April 18, 1996) | 172
Strength in Unity (September 27, 1996) | 175
South Kivu Is Attacked by Rwanda Today (October 11, 1996) | 177
Open Letter (October 13, 1996) | 180
The University of Bukavu and Peace (October 19, 1996) | 182
Remain Strong in Love (October 27, 1996) | 186

Bibliography | 189
Index | 193

Acknowledgments

THIS COLLECTION HAS BENEFITED from the generous assistance of many individuals. Father Alain Nzadi-a-Nzadi, SJ, editor of *Congo-Afrique* and director of CEPAS (Center for the Study of Social Action, Kinshasa), provided permission to include Munzihirwa's *Zaïre-Afrique* writings. Father Rigobert Kyungu Musenge, SJ, provincial of the Jesuits in Central Africa, has been a supporter of this project from the beginning, and provided permission to include selections from Munzihirwa's unpublished writings. Charlie Collier at Wipf and Stock has offered invaluable support and editorial assistance throughout this project. Thanks also to Shannon Carter, E.J. Davila, Savanah N. Landerholm, Elisabeth Rickard, and Matt Wimer for all of their help in bringing this book to print.

Parts of this research were funded through the generous support of a Loyola University Maryland summer research grant. A version of the introduction was presented at the eighth annual Stratton Conference hosted by the Ashland Center for Nonviolence. The feedback provided by those in attendance, as well as conversation with Peter Slade and Craig Hovey, was helpful in making final revisions.

This book is indebted to a growing community of Munzihirwa scholars whose research over the past two decades has significantly advanced understanding of his life and work. Especially helpful in preparing this collection was the scholarship of André Cnockaert, SJ, Philippe de Dorlodot, Emmanuel Katongole, Jean-Marie Vianney Kitumaini, Gauthier Malulu Lock, SJ, Joseph Mukabalera, and Sébastien-Joseph Muyengo Mulombe. Thanks also to the Archdiocese of Bukavu and its Interdiocesan Pastoral Center of Catechesis and Liturgy, which has become a leading center of inquiry regarding Munzihirwa and his legacy.

I want to express a particular debt of gratitude to Irene Safi Turner. Irene grew up in Bukavu and heard Munzihirwa preach from the pulpit

ACKNOWLEDGMENTS

of the Cathedral of Our Lady of Peace. She wrote her doctoral dissertation on Munzihirwa's leadership and influence on the dynamics of conflict in Congo. Our mutual interest in Munzihirwa brought us into contact at the early stages of this project, and Irene's input helped to shape the overall vision and structure of the book. As the project evolved, she remained an invaluable conversation partner, generously making time to field translation questions, explain local references, and provide feedback on the introduction and notes. Her friendship and insight have been instrumental to this book, and I am deeply grateful.

I also want to thank my wife, Ana, and our three boys, Austin, Hunter, and Thomas. They gave me the gift of time when I needed it, and their love and support has been a constant throughout this project. The process of translating Munzihirwa's writings from French has deepened my gratitude for the teachers who first introduced me to the French language, Lucy Bly and Donna Dimery, as well as many Congolese friends and colleagues who have patiently conversed with me in French over the years, especially Kalisa Basara, Katho Bungishabako, and Mike and Bijou Upio.

This book is dedicated to the people of Bukavu. Munzihirwa served as archbishop of Bukavu for the final two years of his life, and during this time he worked alongside the Church and the broader civil society to navigate one of the most difficult periods in the history of the city and region. Countless Bukavu residents, from his immediate successor Emmanuel Kataliko to the Nobel laureate Denis Mukwege, have claimed Munzihirwa as an inspiration. They in turn are the inspiration for spreading his message to a wider audience.

Introduction

THIS COLLECTION OFFERS THE first English translation and compilation of the essential writings of Christophe Munzihirwa, SJ. Munzihirwa was a Congolese Jesuit priest and archbishop whose life spanned many of the seismic events of twentieth-century African history, from decolonization and independence to the democratization movements of the early 1990s and the 1994 Rwandan genocide. Munzihirwa was installed as archbishop of Bukavu in eastern Congo shortly before hundreds of thousands of Rwandan refugees poured into his archdiocese and the surrounding area, seeking relief from famine, disease, and reprisal killings in the aftermath of the genocide. Their numbers would eventually swell to over one million, destabilizing the region and stoking fears of impending war. Munzihirwa quickly became the refugees' most ardent defender, spearheading relief efforts, pressuring local government and military officials, and authoring a fierce letter-writing campaign that reached as far as the secretary general of the United Nations and multiple foreign heads of state. In the end, his impassioned pleas for a peaceful resolution to the crisis went unheeded, and when Rwandan-supported rebels launched the war he tried so hard to prevent, he was among its first victims, assassinated in a square that now bears his name.

Revered as a martyr in eastern Congo, Munzihirwa remains largely unknown in the English-speaking world. This book aims to make his writings accessible to a wider audience. Gathering his major articles, homilies, letters, and other reflections, it surveys Munzihirwa's thought from his political and social analyses of Congolese life under the Mobutu regime to his theological and spiritual reflections on Christian discipleship and the role of the church in modern African society. It culminates with the absorbing writings of the refugee crisis. Engaging such topics as democracy, development, nationalism, enculturation, the rights of refugees, and the ethics of war and peace, these writings introduce readers to Munzihirwa's moral, political, and theological outlook, as well as the Jesuit, Catholic spirituality that fueled his activism. In the process, this book deepens our understanding of one of twentieth-century Africa's most fascinating religious leaders and champions of justice and peace.

The collection is organized into three parts. Part 1, "Development, Democracy, and Citizenship," gathers several of the articles Munzihirwa published in the Kinshasa-based Jesuit journal *Zaïre-Afrique* in the 1980s and early 1990s. Written during the waning years of the dictatorship of Joseph-Désiré Mobutu, these articles take us inside the struggle for democracy and dignity at a time when the Catholic Church served as one of the country's primary voices of opposition to a regime notorious for corruption and self-enrichment. Presaging the kind of prophetic social criticism that later characterizes his refugee activism, these writings witness Munzihirwa fleshing out his vision of a fully enculturated, civic-minded African Catholicism, one that plays a leading role in promoting moral renewal and societal reform. These writings also lend valuable insight into Munzihirwa's many sources, including Christian theology, Catholic social teaching, African culture and tradition, and a wide range of political and social theorists.

The second part, "The Christian Life," turns to Munzihirwa's spiritual and pastoral writings. In devotional meditations, homilies, pastoral letters, and other writings, Munzihirwa examines the shape of Christian discipleship in the Congolese context. Written in a more ecclesial and spiritual key, these writings offer an intimate glimpse into not only his theological commitments, but also his spiritual practice, at the center of which was his deep and abiding identification with the paschal mystery of Christ.[1] For Munzihirwa, journeying into the mystery of a God who suffers with humanity entailed entering into deeper solidarity with the suffering of others. In the face of political injustice, military abuse, and poverty, Christians could find hope in a God who not only suffers with them, but also provides a path of liberating love and transformation. In these writings, Munzihirwa treats a variety of related themes, including the church, family, education, and episcopal leadership. Many of the hallmarks of Jesuit spirituality are evident here as well, including self-examination, discernment, and contemplation, which Munzihirwa creatively adapted and contextualized in response to the challenges and opportunities around him.

---

1. See Emmanuel Katongole's discussion of this in "Christopher Munzihirwa and the Politics of Nonviolent Love," in *Born from Lament*, 164–78.

INTRODUCTION

The third section gathers Munzihirwa's writings from the final chapter of his life, the Rwandan refugee crisis. From the arrival of the first refugees in July 1994 to the start of the first Congo war and ultimately his assassination in 1996, Munzihirwa served as one of the most vocal civil society actors advocating for the rights of refugees and a peaceful resolution to the crisis. This section includes his many letters to domestic and international leaders, as well as homilies, addresses, and pastoral letters that lay out his understanding of how Christian hospitality and neighbor love can defuse tensions and create an atmosphere more conducive to justice and peace. Combining documentary reporting, social critique, and theological analysis, Munzihirwa tirelessly drew attention to the conditions of refugees and the abuses that they and their Congolese hosts suffered at the hands of military actors. As the situation intensified, Munzihirwa outlined a clear strategy for resolving the crisis, calling for voluntary repatriation, political reform in Rwanda, and accountability for genocide perpetrators. His final letters offer a harrowing glimpse inside one leader's experience of a city under siege, and how Munzihirwa sought to maintain a sense of calm and order when most of the political authorities had abandoned the region. "Remain strong in love," he urged the people of Bukavu in his last appeal: "our greatest weapon is love."

Beyond introducing Munzihirwa to a new English readership, the readings gathered here offer much that will be relevant to scholars and students of African theology, African studies, Christian ethics, peace studies, refugee studies, the ethics of war and peace, and other fields. Munzihirwa's writings allow us to grasp the strategic role that religious leaders can play in promoting democratic accountability and social reform, especially in contexts of weakened or collapsed states. These writings also illumine how theological and spiritual sources can inform advocacy efforts for refugees and other vulnerable groups, in addition to outlining specific nonviolent strategies for addressing political, humanitarian, and related crises. Munzihirwa's constructive synthesis of African sources, including most notably his native Bashi culture, with other social, political, and theological sources, speaks directly to discussions of enculturation and decolonization in contemporary African theology. Moreover, his Jesuit, Catholic identity offers a rich window into the diverse expressions of this tradition in the modern world, particularly in the Francophone African context.

Like Oscar Romero, to whom he is often compared, Munzihirwa was an extraordinary leader whose courageous actions at the end of his life define his legacy.² It is easy for such exceptional courage to eclipse all that led up to it: the many years of ordinary formation, thinking, trial, and error that gradually shaped Munzihirwa into the leader he became. The writings in this volume have been selected with an eye to illumining this deeper background, conveying something of Munzihirwa's longer journey: the thinkers, issues, themes, and other formative sources and experiences that were part of his evolution and development. Not all of us may be called to, or be capable of, the sacrifices that Munzihirwa made, but we can all relate to some aspect of the Munzihirwa who emerges from these writings, someone who claimed—and was claimed by—many communities and traditions, trying as best he could, in the contingency of his circumstances, to find a way to live in a manner consistent with his convictions. Here is a citizen who tried to follow his conscience. The many lessons his writings offer, including the importance of truth-telling in democratic society, the role of spirituality in sustaining activism, and the peril of ignoring the voices and experiences of refugees and other marginalized groups, are as essential today as they were in his own time.

To help situate the writings that follow, the remainder of this introduction provides further background on Munzihirwa's life and context. It reviews Munzihirwa's early biography, from his birth and education to his priestly formation and graduate training. It then unpacks the broader context of the Catholic Church under the Mobutu regime, tracking Munzihirwa's emergence as Catholic intellectual, state critic, and church leader. It then considers the major themes of his *Zaïre-Afrique* and spiritual writings, before turning to the climatic events of the refugee crisis. A summary of Munzihirwa's writings and engagement during this period follows, culminating with his final days, assassination, and the immediate aftermath. The discussion concludes with a consideration of Munzihirwa's legacy and the efforts that are currently underway to formally beatify Munzihirwa.

EARLY LIFE AND CONTEXT

Christophe Munzihirwa Mwene Ngabo was born in 1926 in the village of Lukombo, located in the territory of Walungu, in the eastern Congolese province of South Kivu.³ He attended minor seminary near the provincial

---

2. For a comparison of Munzihirwa and Romero, see Mukabalera, "Monseigneur Christophe Munzihirwa, Romero du Congo?"

3. Background information on Munzihirwa is drawn from the following sources:

capital of Bukavu, and major seminary in Nyakibanda, Rwanda, and Moba, Congo.[4] He was ordained a priest on August 17, 1958.[5]

After serving as a diocesan priest for several years, Munzihirwa decided to enter the Society of Jesus in 1963. His Jesuit training took him west to Kinshasa, and later to Europe, where he studied at the St. Albert the Great Philosophical and Theological College in Louvain, Belgium.[6] An avid student of African history and culture, particularly that of his Bashi people, Munzihirwa pursued a master's degree in social science, writing his thesis on the socio-economic position of peasants in his home region of the Kivus. After he pronounced his final vows in 1975, he pursued doctoral studies in sociology in Lumbumbashi and Belgium, using his research to immerse himself in the history of the Bashi, particularly the customs, myths, and practices surrounding the traditional Kabare monarchy.[7]

Had leadership opportunities not called him away from his studies, Munzihirwa would have likely gone on to a successful academic career. But in 1978, he was appointed rector of the St. Peter Canisius Jesuit Faculty of Philosophy in Kimwenza, setting in motion his rapid rise through the ranks of regional Jesuit and Catholic leadership.[8] In 1980, the superior general of the Society of Jesus, Pedro Arrupe, SJ, appointed Munzihirwa provincial of the Jesuit Province of Central Africa, a post that entailed overseeing the order's activities in Congo, Rwanda, and Burundi.[9] In 1986, Munzihirwa

---

Amoussou, "Munzihirwa, Christophe, SJ," 533–34; Cnockaert, *In Memoriam*, 4–27; Katongole, "Christopher Munzihirwa and the Politics of Nonviolent Love," 164–78; Mirindi, *Père Evêque Christophe Munzihirwa Mwene Ngabo, S.J.*, 2–19; and Kyungu, *Liberté interieure comme fruit du discernment spirituel*.

4. Farhi, "Mzee Christophe Munzihirwa Mwene Ngabo," in Cnockaert, *In Memoriam*, 4.

5. Farhi, "Mzee Christophe Munzihirwa Mwene Ngabo," in Cnockaert, *In Memoriam*, 4. See also Kyungu's discussion of Munzihirwa's spiritual formation in *Liberté interieure comme fruit*, 59–76.

6. Farhi, "Mzee Christophe Munzihirwa Mwene Ngabo," in Cnockaert, *In Memoriam*, 4.

7. For more on the influence of Bashi culture upon Munzihirwa, see Mukabalera, "Monseigneur Christophe Munzihirwa, Romero du Congo?," 15–20; and Kyungu, *Liberté interieure comme fruit*, 191–244. A portion of Munzihirwa's doctoral research was published posthumously as "Pouvoir royal et ideologies: role du mythe, des rites et des proverbs dans la monarchie précoloniale du royaume de Kabaré (Zaïre)."

8. Farhi, "Mzee Christophe Munzihirwa Mwene Ngabo," in Cnockaert, *In Memoriam*, 4.

9. Kyungu, *Liberté interieure comme fruit*, 77–78.

was named auxiliary bishop of the diocese of Kasongo, becoming bishop of that diocese in 1990.[10]

Munzihirwa ascended the ranks of a Catholic Church which had become, by the 1980s and early 1990s, one of the main voices of opposition to the Mobutu regime.[11] Joseph-Désiré Mobutu took power through a military coup in 1965 after several volatile years following Congo's independence from Belgium in 1960. Intent upon charting a new course, he re-named the country Zaire and implemented several ambitious programs, including an economic plan, Zairianization, that placed foreign-owned companies under state control, and an *authenticité* campaign that sought to promote indigenous self-expression and root out colonial influence.[12]

Mobutu regarded the Catholic Church as one of those influences, and banned the use of Christian names, imposed state oversight over Christian schools and universities, and limited public expressions of Christian faith.[13] The Church's newfound marginal status allied it more closely to the people it served, who found the Church a more reliable partner than the state, whose fiscal policies quickly failed and whose governance became increasingly characterized by violent repression and corruption.[14] Leaders such as the archbishop of Kinshasa, Cardinal Joseph-Albert Malula, and the archbishop of Lubumbashi, Eugéne Kabanga Songasonga, became openly critical of the regime, and the Church eventually played a key role in pressuring Mobutu to concede to a democratization process in the early 1990s, with then-Archbishop of Kisangani Laurent Monsengwo Pasinya serving as the president of the Sovereign National Conference.[15]

Munzihirwa followed in this line of outward-facing, civic-minded church leaders who did not shy away from criticizing the Mobutu state. In

---

10. Farhi, "Mzee Christophe Munzihirwa Mwene Ngabo," in Cnockaert, *In Memoriam*, 5.

11. For background on the relationship between the Catholic Church and the Zairian state during the Mobutu era, see Young and Turner, *Rise and Decline of the Zairian State*; Oyatambwe, *Eglise catholique et pouvoir politique au Congo-Zaïre*; Okitembo, *Engagement politique de l'Église catholique au Zaïre*; and Prunier, "Catholic Church and the Kivu Conflict," 139–62.

12. Young and Turner, *Rise and Decline of the Zairian State*, 63–71; Prunier, "Catholic Church and the Kivu Conflict," 142.

13. Young and Turner, *Rise and Decline of the Zairian State*, 68; Prunier, "Catholic Church and the Kivu Conflict," 142.

14. Prunier, "Catholic Church and the Kivu Conflict," 142.

15. Young and Turner, *Rise and Decline of the Zairian State*, 67–73; Prunier, "Catholic Church and the Kivu Conflict," 142–45.

the early 1970s, Munzihirwa was a graduate student at the University of Zaire, where he also served as a student chaplain. The students launched a protest against the regime, and Mobutu responded by closing the university and conscripting the students. As a priest, Munzihirwa could have claimed exemption from the required military service, but he joined the students anyway. When Cardinal Malula won an appeal for Munzihirwa's release, Munzihirwa refused the offer, opting to remain with the students for several months before returning to his priestly duties.[16] In the coming years, he would only grow more vocal in his criticism.

THE *ZAÏRE-AFRIQUE* WRITINGS

In the 1980s, Munzihirwa became a regular contributor to *Zaïre-Afrique*, a Jesuit-run journal that published Catholic perspectives on politics and society. In these articles, Munzihirwa developed his critique of the Mobutu regime, taking specific aim at its claims to *authenticité*. Drawing upon his extensive studies of African history and culture, Munzihirwa argued that the regime's construction of *authenticité* reflected only a partial, highly ideological rendering of African tradition, one that intentionally minimized or evaded elements of tradition that stood in clear conflict with its practices. Nothing in Munzihirwa's studies suggested there was anything authentically African about dictatorship or kleptocracy. Extending the point beyond Zaire, he asked, "What should we make of the contemporary situation in African countries? These countries are poor, and their leaders are often rich; these monarchs affirm they come from a line of traditional leaders who distribute their wealth. Today's leaders take the lion's share of the country's wealth. They justify their kleptocracy with an appeal to *authenticité*."[17] Yet "upon closer inspection," Munzihirwa observed, "today's regimes are neither a reflection nor a legacy of the kind of governance practiced by our ancestors."[18]

Munzihirwa pointed to such traditional practices as the *palaver* and elder council, which prized democratic consensus and checks on power. In the great stories passed down through the generations, the king was depicted as "a symbol of justice, of concern for the least of these, a living law

---

16. Farhi, "Mzee Christophe Munzihirwa Mwene Ngabo," in Cnockaert, *In Memoriam*, 4.

17. "Great Palaver We Call the National Conference," 80.

18. "Democracy: What Kind? What For?," 64.

and guarantor of the people's happiness. If natural disasters and famines repeatedly occurred, the people would naturally wonder if the king truly had the ancestors' blessing."[19] "All of this," Munzihirwa concluded, "indicates to us that a modern power that wants to be authentic cannot be content merely to watch over the territory, but must commit to a fuller realization of justice, and promote economic policies that allow the people to provide for themselves and develop."[20]

Munzihirwa extended this critique of *authenticité* to the regime's characterization of Christianity. On Mobutu's terms, Christianity was little more than a colonial holdover, something that inhibited authentic African expression. But as Munzihirwa saw it, the opposite was the case: "The hope that the resurrected Christ brings us is the hope of the personal, collective, and total liberation of man."[21] A fully enculturated African Catholicism could make a vital contribution to the flourishing of African identity and the promotion of the common good, as the Church's own prophetic stance against Mobutu witnessed. Munzihirwa put it in these terms:

> True Christianity is an opiate for no one: not the people, the rich, or the intellectuals. On the contrary, it keeps us from sleeping, arousing and maintaining a perpetual dissatisfaction. It is a principle of ongoing openness to God's will for individuals, institutions, and societies bogged down in the surrounding materialism. Because it tirelessly demands truth, it summons individuals and institutions, every moment of every day, before the secret tribunal of conscience, where all witnesses are held accountable. Next to these demands, traditional or so-called revolutionary justice appears artificial, imposed in a way that stifles questions and thus its own project of *authenticité* and revolution.[22]

For Munzihirwa, the Mobutu regime's claim to revolutionary *authenticité* was belied by its suppression of a religion that promoted the kind of questioning and accountability that any commitment to social change requires. "A truly fruitful, creative revolution can only be accomplished by appealing to what is best in man and inspiring his righteous and generous passions," Munzihirwa observed.[23] Quoting Péguy's famous saying, "the

---

19. "Great Palaver We Call the National Conference," 80.
20. "Great Palaver We Call the National Conference," 80.
21. "For a Christian, What Is Development?," 41.
22. "Cultural Traditions and Socio-Economic Development," 59-60.
23. "Democracy: What Kind? What For?," 68.

social revolution will be moral or it will not be a revolution," Munzihirwa expanded, "We cannot transform the social system without first reforming ourselves, stirring within ourselves a spiritual and moral awakening. This entails digging down to the personal, spiritual, and moral foundations of human life, renewing the spiritual and moral ideas that constitute, and continue to inspire, the life of the social group as such—in short, giving the group a new sense of purpose."[24]

Throughout his *Zaïre-Afrique* writings, Munzihirwa made the case for what an enculturated African Catholicism could bring to such moral and civic renewal. In his essays on development, for example, Munzihirwa observed that while theories of development abound, few actually specified the overall ends of development. "International policies regarding the division of labor, the easing of the population burden, the idealization of isolated cultures, the dissemination and/or transfer of appropriate technologies all capture partial truths about man and international society, but are they grounded in the same love for life in its fullness? What happiness do they envision? And for whom?"[25] Development goals, Munzihirwa found, were often framed in strictly immanent terms, neglecting the spiritual and transcendent dimensions of human life. He pointed out that in many African traditions, individual or communal well-being could not adequately be conceived apart from one's relationship to the ancestors: "Our customs have never considered death an endpoint, a door to nothingness. The happiness of the deceased seems to depend upon the rapport he or she maintains with the world of the living. . . . At the same time, the happiness of those who are on this earth is related to the life of those who are gone. This is a fundamental consideration that our development policies cannot neglect."[26] Munzihirwa also emphasized how the eternal perspective of Christianity imparted to social life a sense of moral purpose and forward-looking hope. "Development for a Christian is a dynamic that promotes people rather than riches, human solidarity rather than solitary individuals. It regards human beings not as ephemeral creatures doomed to oblivion, but a multitude that participates in a web of unlimited relationships, in this life and the next, animated by the One who is, in essence, Relation and Love."[27]

---

24. "Democracy: What Kind? What For?," 70.
25. "For a Christian, What Is Development?," 40-41.
26. "For a Christian, What Is Development?," 33.
27. "For a Christian, What Is Development?," 41-42.

As the democratization movement gained momentum in the early 1990s, Munzihirwa also wrote extensively on democracy. "True democracy," Munzihirwa writes, "entails moving towards greater freedom, and towards greater equality through freedom. This process involves all levels of society: it complements the freedom of autonomy, or the absence of physical or intellectual constraints, with the freedom of participation, the direct involvement of the governed in the exercise of power."[28] This freedom of participation, included, crucially, a commitment to fostering a culture of truth. "To protect [freedom] against arbitrary power, individuals must participate in the functioning of government not only through the right to vote, but also through freedom of opinion, which requires true information."[29] The experience of living under the Mobutu regime sensitized Munzihirwa to the ways dictatorships rely upon various forms of untruth, most notably ideology, to legitimate and augment their power. "Placing itself at the service of this ideology, a government can claim the right to absolute power because it knows everything. It rules absolutely in order to force its subjects to recognize that reality does indeed accord with the ideology embodied by the man or group who purports to know and control it. It imposes its so-called truth in order to silence any approach that would shed a different light on events. It ultimately obscures the truth."[30]

The strength of democracy, as Munzihirwa saw it, was precisely its capacity to facilitate multiple viewpoints and various mechanisms for arriving at truth and identifying error. Speaking truth to power was an essential check on that power. "Mistakes are inevitable in a democracy, but democracy can facilitate individual and social growth when it does not repeat the same mistakes and strives to do better. This is the role that freedom of information, investigation, and verification play in arriving at justifiable opinions, benefiting society and enabling it to advance towards truth and solidarity with dignity."[31]

It is hard to overstate how important this link between democracy and truth was for Munzihirwa. Truth-telling was for him a vital form of public engagement. Whether it was contesting the Mobutu regime's claims to *authenticité*, describing the everyday abuses and indignities suffered by Congolese citizens at the hands of the police or military, or later, drawing

28. "Democracy: What Kind? What For?," 74.
29. "Great Palaver We Call the National Conference," 77.
30. "Democracy: What Kind? What For?," 68-69.
31. "Democracy: What Kind? What For?," 69.

INTRODUCTION

the world's attention to the plight of the Rwandan refugees and the threat of looming war, he used his platform as a church leader to shine a light on the realities facing the people in his region.

Munzihirwa had no illusions about what such a commitment entailed. It entailed risk. It entailed struggle. Throughout the *Zaïre-Afrique* writings, he comes back to the basic struggle that all gains in development, democracy, and other areas of life require:

> When we look at the history of the West, we see that civil and human rights have only been won through great struggle. The religious formation of conscience and the mystical shocks of holiness have played no small part in these gains. But it's important to note that these gains are not attributable to a conversion of elites. Western society has been called to account and brought to heel, in large part, by the poor, who have become more aware, more willing to resist, and more adept in their organization.[32]

Munzihirwa believed that it was ordinary citizens who were the main drivers of social change. In Zaire/Congo, the capacity of citizens to drive such change had been held back for too long by a regime that inhibited individual and collective agency. "We must rid ourselves of the predatory spirit of gathering what we have not sown, hunting what we have not raised, and cutting down what we have not planted. . . When we do not replant, we do not transform, and we do not take part in history."[33] This is a message he believed found a resounding echo in the Christian tradition:

> To be effective, our Christian commitment to integral development must be realistic and take into account this international struggle for existence, a struggle for the true values of humanity, interconnection, and openness to the transcendent. We must believe that our efforts can bring about change. We must believe in ourselves. Christian hope, born from the memory of Christ crucified and resurrected, leads us to hope when there is no hope. It does not see the future of man and society with a naive optimism, sweetly dreaming of a possible future. On the contrary, it sees it with the acceptance of the struggle it will demand.[34]

---

32. "Cultural Traditions and Socio-Economic Development," 60.
33. "Cultural Traditions and Socio-Economic Development," 62.
34. "For a Christian, What Is Development?," 38-39.

Here Munzihirwa gestures towards the deeper spiritual and theological sources that Christians can draw upon as they take up this struggle. For more on these sources, we turn to his spiritual and pastoral writings.

THE SPIRITUAL AND PASTORAL WRITINGS

Munzihirwa's writings spanned many genres and audiences, reflecting the different stages of his ministry and the populations he served. In addition to his *Zaïre-Afrique* writings, he wrote numerous homilies and pastoral letters that applied church teaching and liturgically inspired themes to the challenges and aspirations of his parishioners and the wider public. Munzihirwa also wrote personal meditations reflecting upon his own Jesuit, Catholic spiritual practice. Selections from these writings are included in the second part of this book.

The section opens with a meditation Munzihirwa wrote on the twenty-fifth anniversary of his ordination, in which he poignantly revisits the reasons he joined the priesthood. Citing 1 Pet 4:13, "But rejoice insofar as you participate in the sufferings of Christ, so that you may also be glad and shout for joy when his glory is revealed,"[35] he reflects, "Before my ordination, I wanted this passage to guide my path. For many years since I have asked Christ to give me the grace to keep this message close to my heart."[36] The mystery of a God who becomes incarnate, suffers, and rises from the dead, who offers disciples a way of uniting their struggles to God's own and find a transformative path through them, stays with Munzihirwa, recurring as a central motif in his writings.[37] In his "Paschal Meditation," he directly identifies the Congolese struggle for dignity and recognition with the way of the cross, commenting, "we have a companion who knows the way well: he is the Way. Amid the plunder, poverty, and oppression that swirl around us, we must find internal peace in him, in the hope that God will not abandon us."[38] In his 1994 Lenten letter, he returns to the theme, enjoining his readers "to participate in the trial of Christ" and place their "trust in the One who is the Way, Life and Truth. Let us try to take on the

---

35. Editor's translation of Munzihirwa's original.

36. "Meditation on the Anniversary of My Ordination," 83.

37. On the centrality of the "way of Christ" in Munzihirwa's thought, see Katongole, "Christopher Munzihirwa and the Politics of Nonviolent Love," 173–74.

38. "Paschal Meditation," 86.

feelings of his heart, he who, in Jesus, was despised and did not despise, who was oppressed by violence and did not oppress: he loved."[39]

For Munzihirwa, to participate in the sufferings of Christ was not to accept passively one's condition, but to participate in a different way of being in the world, one defined by nonviolence and love.[40] In his 1994 Christmas letter, Munzihirwa writes, "To realize his purpose, Jesus does not employ his enemies' tactics, but asks Herod gently: 'Why do you want to kill me?'; the soldier who slaps him, 'Why do you hit me?'; Saul of Tarsus, 'Why do you persecute me?'"[41] God chooses weakness over strength, vulnerability over brute force: "God starts his great works modestly, with no *coup d'état* or referendum. . . [he] enters our world where no one or nearly no one expected him: in a lost place, in a poor and unknown family, in a setting of little importance, at a time when his nation was colonized by the Romans."[42] To embrace such weakness and vulnerability inevitably brings one into conflict with the powers that be; as Munzihirwa puts it, "the shadow of the cross is already cast over the manger. And it will not stop expanding until the day when the political leaders crucify, as a vulgar agitator, the only begotten Son of God, who came into the world to save it."[43]

The spiritual writings provide valuable insight into Munzihirwa's many sources of moral inspiration, particularly those figures he thought epitomized this cruciform way in the world. They range from the second-century martyr Felicity to the late-nineteenth-/early-twentieth-century Congolese saint Isidore Bakanja.[44] No inspiration looms larger over these pages than Mary.[45] For Munzihirwa, Mary "embodied the kind of presence

---

39. "Cry of the Poor: On the Occasion of Lent," 93.

40. Katongole captures this when he writes, "But just as with the wailings of Jeremiah and Jesus, Munzihirwa's anguished life points to a revolutionary social vision founded on nonviolent, self-sacrificing love. . . . The church's own ability to be such a nonviolent interruption depends on its ability to enter the 'way of Christ'—to enter, that is, the way of God's self-sacrificing love that is manifested through his suffering and death. As it turns out, entering the 'way of Christ' is not a mere pious or spiritual recommendation; it is an invitation into a revolutionary social vision" ("Christopher Munzihirwa and the Politics of Nonviolent Love," 166).

41. "Christmas: A Challenge to Human Plans," 107.

42. "Christmas: A Challenge to Human Plans," 105.

43. "Christmas: A Challenge to Human Plans," 106.

44. See, in this volume, his 1995 New Year pastoral letter and his homily on the occasion of his installation as archbishop of Bukavu.

45. On the theme of Marian devotion in Munzihirwa's thought, see Mirindi, *Père Evêque Christophe Munzihirwa Mwene Ngabo, S.J.*, 36–39.

that Jesus sought from his disciples in the garden of Gethsemane. Despised with her son, she did not despise; crushed with the pain of witnessing her son martyred, she still had the courage to accept a new mission of love."[46] Whereas the disciples fell asleep in the garden, Mary "returns to keep watch. And there, at dawn on the third day, she receives the happy news: Jesus is alive."[47] For Christians, Mary is not simply a moral exemplar, but their active intercessor, spurring them on to a likeminded faithfulness: "Let us watch with Mary from now on, and more intensely, from Good Friday to Easter dawn. Let us watch like her, with a heart that refuses to stop loving."[48]

This theme of watching recalls Munzihirwa's earlier appeals to Christian conscience in the *Zaïre-Afrique* writings and his understanding of Christianity not as a sleep-inducing opiate, but a morally alert and active form of civic engagement. It is thus not surprising that he makes the theme of watching the central one of his installation homily as archbishop of Bukavu. Munzihirwa likens the role of the bishop precisely to a watchman, observing:

> Being a bishop means being a watchman, night and day. The watchman's task is to warn when a thief, an enemy arrives. Like the watchman, the bishop listens. He watches and surveys. He is always on alert. He must keep the brigands, the sowers of discord, the "wolves" dressed in sheep's clothing, from entering and harming his flock. Do not be surprised that the bishop, like a watchman, is committed to his work, to the duty of his office. He is required to do so.[49]

Munzihirwa delivered this homily as the Rwandan genocide and its aftershocks were exploding across the border, anticipating how it would spill over into his country and bring with it numerous armed groups seeking to exploit the situation for their gain. The people of Bukavu would later take to calling Munzihirwa *Zamu* or *Muhudumu*, their "watchman," in recognition of the way he fulfilled the role he set out for himself at the outset of his ministry among them.[50]

---

46. "Cry of the Poor: On the Occasion of Lent," 94.
47. "Cry of the Poor: On the Occasion of Lent," 94.
48. "Cry of the Poor: On the Occasion of Lent," 94.
49. "Homily from Installation as Archbishop of Bukavu," 102.
50. See Jean-Baptiste Kabazane Nsibula Orhaaciyuma, "Sentinelle de Bukavu," in Cnockaert, *In Memoriam*, 20–21; Katongole, "Christopher Munzihirwa and the Politics of Nonviolent Love," 170–71.

INTRODUCTION

Munzihirwa's spiritual and pastoral writings also consider such topics as the family and education. In "On the Year of the Family," Munzihirwa weighs the cumulative effect of nearly thirty years of Mobutu's rule upon the country. "After what we have been through, 'unity' has enabled the internal plundering of a state where no one really feels responsible for life or its goods."[51] Individuals "live merely side by side, instead of promoting a spirit of responsibility, complementarity, and tolerance."[52] Munzihirwa believed the family had a crucial role to play here. "Faith and justice can only be preserved when they are deepened and spread. They are deepened when rooted in the basic structure of the family. This is where nature meets culture. This is where early formation takes place, influencing the whole life of a human person, and even social, economic and political institutions."[53] Inculcating virtue and building character, the family could promote broader social and political renewal. "A conscience trained in personal and social responsibility by the family can help foster a state that truly is a public thing—a Republic—where everyone feels involved and can promote their own destiny, where each person can open his or her heart to international dimensions, to eternal dimensions, by learning tolerance and forgiveness of the enemy."[54]

Munzihirwa saw a throughline from the family to schools. "And our schools? They are the necessary complement to the formation of the citizen, provided they are 'educational settings,' permitting young people to live together without discrimination of any kind, broadening their sense of belonging beyond the family to a social community, a homeland . . . the surrounding nation which permits all ethnic groups to live together."[55] This vision of the school as a space in which one encounters difference and broadens one's sense of belonging is integral to Munzihirwa's vision of education. In one of his final addresses, "The University of Bukavu and Peace," Munzihirwa explicitly connects this theme to higher education, arguing that embedded in the idea of the university is an aspiration to "universality," a commitment to all cultures and peoples coming together to learn from one another: "It was a vision of dialogue across ethnicities that informed its sense of universality. . . . The greatness of a university, like a nation, comes

51. "On the Year of the Family," 98.
52. "On the Year of the Family," 98.
53. "On the Year of the Family," 96.
54. "On the Year of the Family," 98-99.
55. "On the Year of the Family," 98.

in knowing how to deal with differences instead of destroying them. This is what drives the spirit of innovation and creativity."[56] That Munzihirwa made this argument at the height of the refugee crisis, when ethnic animosities threatened to engulf the region, only reinforced what he took to be the moral urgency of the university's basic enterprise. From this vantage point, there was a crucial peacebuilding dimension to education, in that it, like the family, helped to cultivate the kind of practices and dispositions that enabled citizens to live more harmoniously with one another.[57]

Finally, Munzihirwa's spiritual and pastoral writings illumine his spiritual practice. Munzihirwa developed a reputation for simplicity, preferring to dress in ordinary clothes and refusing much of the pomp that accompanied the office of archbishop.[58] Simplicity, cruciform living, self-examination, and discernment are just some of the many aspects of Jesuit spirituality that emerge in these writings.[59] Not to be overlooked is Munzihirwa's emphasis upon the practice of silence, the subject of the final selection in this section. "Silence," he writes, "while it may be the opposite of speech, is not devoid of meaning. We manifest a host of feelings by being silent."[60] He discusses the silence of indifference and contempt, as well as the silence of respect, admiration, attention, and intimacy. Elsewhere he also mentions the silence of death, "a word of great richness for those who

---

56. "University of Bukavu and Peace," 182.

57. In this vision of peace as organically constituted by a variety of institutions at different levels (e.g., personal, interpersonal, institutional, societal), Munzihirwa was influenced by Augustine, the theologian whom he cites more than any other. Munzihirwa was particularly fond of Augustine's definition of peace as the "tranquility of order," which he cites in the "University of Bukavu and Peace" address. Other writings in this volume where Munzihirwa draws upon Augustine include his "Paschal Meditation," "Cry of the Poor: On the Occasion of Lent" (February 28, 1994), "Do the Nations Want to Serve the Great Lakes Region of Africa?" (August 3, 1994), and "S.O.S. from the Archbishop of Bukavu on Behalf of the Refugees" (September 8, 1994).

58. Munzihirwa's simplicity is a common theme in many of the tributes offered by fellow Jesuits and colleagues in Cnockaert, *In Memoriam*. Francois-Xavier Mitima, for example, recounts, "He didn't like being taken care of too much. Formalities bothered him to no end" (14). André Kajemba adds, "He didn't want anyone kissing his hand or kneeling as he passed. We would laugh to each other in the office, saying it was his driver who looked like a bishop, not him. I never saw him in a skullcap. Maybe he wore it to Mass. Only his episcopal ring and cross gave him away as a prelate" (23).

59. For more on the influence of Jesuit spirituality upon Munzihirwa, see Kyungu, *Liberté interieure comme fruit*, 245–98; and Lock, *Mgr Christophe Munzihirwa*.

60. "On Silence," 112.

know how to listen from within."[61] The "ability to live with a little silence," Munzihirwa notes, "characterizes the true believer and separates him from the world of unbelief."[62]

THE RWANDAN REFUGEE CRISIS

Pope John Paul II appointed Munzihirwa archbishop of Bukavu on March 27, 1994. Soon after, Munzihirwa traveled to Rome to participate in the Special Assembly for Africa of the Synod of Bishops, which met until early May.[63] Meanwhile, on April 7, the Rwandan genocide began, eventually claiming the lives of an estimated 800,000 Tutsis before the Rwandan Patriotic Front secured Kigali in mid-July 1994.

Most of the genocide perpetrators, including former government soldiers and *Interahamwe*, fled to neighboring countries, including Zaire. Fearing reprisals and repression under the new RPF government, hundreds of thousands of Rwandan Hutus, most of whom did not participate in the genocide, also fled.[64] Some entered Zaire via Goma to the north, while others fled south through Bukavu. Dozens of refugee camps soon appeared across the region. Over one million refugees would eventually enter the country, some 650,000 in and around Munzihirwa's archdiocese of Bukavu.[65]

Over the next two years, Munzihirwa would emerge as one of the most important leaders organizing the civil society response to the crisis in South Kivu.[66] Through homilies, speeches, and countless letters to political leaders, military officials, NGO representatives, and foreign dignitaries, he sought to draw attention to the abuses suffered by refugees and Congolese civilians. He implored the Zairian military to observe restraint and lobbied for a negotiated settlement that would enable a peaceful, voluntary

---

61. "For a Christian, What Is Development?," 32.

62. "On Silence," 113.

63. Farhi, "Mzee Christophe Munzihirwa Mwene Ngabo," in Cnockaert, *In Memoriam*, 5.

64. For an overview of the Rwandan refugee crisis, see Prunier, *Africa's World War*, 24–72; and Stearns, *Dancing in the Glory of Monsters*, 13–90.

65. Prunier, *Africa's World War*, 25.

66. Jean-Marie Vianney Kitumaini provides a helpful overview of Munzihirwa's engagement during the refugee crisis in "L'agir socio-politique de Mgr Christophe Munzihirwa à Bukavu," 204–17.

repatriation and avert war. Selections from these writings are gathered in part 3 of this collection.

Throughout these writings, we see Munzihirwa expanding upon themes from earlier work to illumine the nature of the crisis and guide the local response. "The crisis in Rwanda reveals our own crisis," he wrote in July 1994, drawing attention to the fact that decades of state neglect under Mobutu left Zaire ill-prepared to respond to the situation. "When the mass of refugees arrived, the authorities in Bukavu were completely absent. They only started to show up late, when the conscience of Christians had already been outraged by the behavior of those seeking to take advantage of the vulnerable position of the refugees and confusion in the city."[67] Munzihirwa describes members of the Zairian Civil Guard assaulting refugees and local residents; thieves donning Zairian military uniforms and seizing goods on the bridges at the border; and landlords opportunistically evicting tenants so they can charge higher rents.

In the face of these abuses, Munzihirwa exhorted the Church to extend Christian hospitality to those seeking refuge:

> Disciples of Christ can only claim to be followers of Christ if they have the honesty and courage to be "servants of all," and stand in solidarity with the poor. We are told that love is proven through action. If there are refugees at our doorstep, let us create an atmosphere of compassion where the flowers of mutual assistance can bloom. We must know how to welcome every brother and sister, without distinction of race or social class, without making accusations or showing contempt. If the possibility of refugees returning home emerges, we must be servants of mutual love, dialogue, mercy, and reconciliation at all levels. If a new future of national coexistence is to be born, Christ's disciples must be leaven in the dough; not militants of intolerant parties, but bearers of the Spirit.[68]

In other letters, Munzihirwa deepened the theological dimensions of this appeal. "We Christians cannot forget that Jesus, shortly after he was born, lived as a refugee in Egypt, and that the history of his ancestors included several exiles; we must not forget that Israel came out of slavery in Egypt."[69] Returning specifically to the theme of the paschal mystery of Christ,

---

67. "Homily from Mass for Refugees and the Peace of All (July 24, 1994)," 117.

68. "Do the Nations Want to Serve the Great Lakes Region of Africa? The Church Faces the Challenge of Violence and Hypocrisy (August 3, 1994)," 127.

69. "Homily from Mass for Refugees and the Peace of All," 118.

Munzihirwa identifies the suffering of the refugees with Christ's own, writing, "Since we welcomed you, your fate has in a way become our fate. It is the same Christ who suffers in us all. We therefore cannot accept the measures that have been imposed upon you, which violate your human rights, especially your rights as refugees."[70]

Munzihirwa further challenged his fellow Christians to resist the growing militarization of the region and instead adopt a Christian ethic of love:

> Christians: Even if we cannot prevent violence, we must always disapprove of it; we must know how to say NO, an absolute no to it. Even if we fail to unravel the Gordian knot of hypocrisy, we must always denounce it: we must know how to say NO, an equally absolute no to it as well. Then we must try to overcome the violence and hypocrisy, awakening a better vision of this profoundly troubled world, where the wheat and chaff always grow together.... The good grain is Christ living today in the midst of the chaff, in the darkest hours of human tragedy. It is an attitude that steps back in tolerance, sensitive to the power of love to open the way to disarmament, providing a surer foundation upon which to rebuild.[71]

This notion of a love that opens "the way to disarmament," easing tensions and fostering good will, recurs throughout the writings of this period. In his final Christmas letter, for example, Munzihirwa observes:

> When God becomes a child, he knows that he cannot better express himself than through the weakness of a child. It is a disarmed love. This child's gaze brings us back to the childhood of man, where God keeps saying to us, as he does to his beloved Son, "Today I have begotten you." From now on, we cannot truly look at anyone without seeing this Child-God hidden in the face of every being, who wants to be born there too.[72]

Seeing God in the face of each person, seeing each person as a child of God, changes how we see the world. In Munzihirwa's striking terms, all the world becomes an epiphany:

> Let us open our hearts to receive the Child-Jesus in whom everything is new, he who came to break down the wall that separates

---

70. "Letter to the Refugees (November 18, 1995)," 161.
71. "Do the Nations Want to Serve the Great Lakes Region of Africa?," 124.
72. "Christmas Letter (1995)," 166.

the peoples, to dispel the thick darkness in our hearts. In him, there is neither Jew nor Greek, free man nor slave, neither male nor female, but all are children of the same Father, all sons, one in his only Son, all united with those who suffer. Henceforth, no one can appear in the world without Christ appearing in him and with him. The entire universe, through the hidden power of this child, becomes Epiphany, the manifestation and appearance of Christ. Humanity is no longer a wandering and scattered flock, but a community of the Sons of God. Each of my brothers renews for me the birth of Bethlehem.[73]

As the crisis wore on, Munzihirwa continued to document the deteriorating conditions in the refugee camps and the increasing toll of the crisis upon the local population. The region, he emphasized, was already densely populated before the crisis; supporting over one million refugees now pushed it to the brink. "The people of Bushi have already exhausted their provisions by sharing them with the refugees. . . . Fields ordinarily used for cultivation are currently occupied by the refugees. . . . Several schools have been damaged. . . . Trees need to be replanted everywhere."[74] As for the refugees themselves, "They live under increasingly distressed conditions: the distribution of food occurs sporadically and it is difficult to find wood for cooking. Several humanitarian organizations are leaving."[75] This was before Rwanda and Burundi started blocking World Food Program trucks from entering the camps. "They don't have clothes to wear or food to eat. Now we fear a war of the hungry, especially given that there are many armed young people among them."[76]

Meanwhile, conditions back in Rwanda deterred refugees from returning. "They are afraid of being imprisoned based upon a simple accusation, on unproven facts, or being killed if they try to reclaim their property."[77] In April 1995, thousands of internally displaced Hutus in Rwanda were killed during the Rwandan army's attack on a camp in Kibeho, intensifying fears that a similar fate awaited refugees if they returned.[78] Munzihirwa

73. "Christmas Letter (1995)," 166-67.
74. "Letter to Misereor Representative (September 19, 1994)," 135-36.
75. "Letter to Cardinal Daneels and Monsignor Delaporte (January 16, 1995)," 142.
76. "Social Situation in Bukavu Today (April 28, 1995)," 144.
77. "Letter to Cardinal Daneels and Monsignor Delaporte," 142.
78. The Kibeho massacre occurred April 22, 1995, when the Rwandan Army opened fire on refugees at a camp of internally displaced persons. Rwandan government officials put the death toll at around three hundred, but Gérard Prunier suggests that the number

criticized Western governments and NGOs for not exerting more pressure upon Rwanda and Zaire to find a peaceful resolution to the crisis. He understood that armed genocide perpetrators remained in these camps, launching periodic attacks against Rwanda. He criticized the absentee Zairian government for its inaction. But he also appealed to international actors not to be "manipulated into condemning the Hutus *en bloc*,"[79] arguing that "a Hutu should be distinguished from members of the *Interahamwe* or the presidential guard who sought to maintain power through genocide; so too a Tutsi should be distinguished from certain members of the RPF who want to take power by force and eliminate all opposition."[80] A narrative that criminalized all refugees could make a military solution seem inevitable. Munzihirwa warned that such a solution could lead to years of armed conflict and mass killings of the refugees. He implored all sides to adopt a peacebuilding strategy that involved negotiations between the Rwandan government and refugee leaders; increased humanitarian aid in the camps; accountability for Hutu genocide perpetrators; an end to arbitrary arrests, detentions, and killings inside Rwanda; a halt to the arms trade; and ultimately a safe, voluntary repatriation for the refugees.[81]

The Zairian military did not help the situation by preying upon its own people. Munzihirwa appealed directly to military leaders, asking, "Why are Zairians in general afraid of the military, when the soldier is their brother? Why do they fear him rather than love him? It is because bad soldiers are tarnishing the image of the army."[82] Refugees were "continually hassled and robbed of their belongings," while Zairian citizens were unable to move freely in the city, encountering multiple checkpoints where they had to pay numerous taxes and bear the burden of supporting soldiers who went unpaid by the government.[83]

Munzihirwa held up Congo's own military past as a standard for these undisciplined soldiers to emulate. Referring to the Congolese soldiers who contributed to Allied victories in Ethiopia during WWII, Munzihirwa

---

could have been as high as five thousand. See Prunier, *Africa's World War*, 41.

79. "Letter to Misereor Representative," 136.

80. "Do the Nations Want to Serve the Great Lakes Region of Africa?," 126.

81. See especially his second letter to UN Secretary General Boutros Boutros-Ghali and letter to former US president Jimmy Carter in this volume.

82. "Homily from Mass at Saio Military Camp (October 15, 1994)," 138.

83. "Letter to the Chief of Staff of the Zairian Armed Forces (FAZ), Major General Eluki Monga Aundu (November 6, 1995)," 156.

observed, "Let the army currently stationed in Kivu ask itself: Could you achieve the victory at Saio? At Asosa? Gambela? Could you save us?"[84] He also mentioned national heroes who helped put down internal rebellions in the 1960s. To this he added numerous scriptural passages on military discipline, underscoring John the Baptist's instruction to soldiers, "Do no violence or harm to anyone and be content with your wages."[85]

Such letters illumine Munzihirwa's broader views on the ethics of war and peace. While he was in general opposed to war and strongly opposed a military solution to the refugee crisis, he acknowledged a state's right to self-defense, quoting the words of *Gaudium et Spes*: "as long as the danger of war remains and there is no competent and sufficiently powerful authority at the international level, governments cannot be denied the right to legitimate defense once every means of peaceful settlement has been exhausted."[86] But this was no *carte blanche*. Being a soldier entailed enormous responsibility, and could only be understood as a service to the common good. Addressing himself to soldiers, Munzihirwa said, "To defend the country, you first have to love it, from its youngest to oldest members, then be trained in the necessary discipline and skill to defend them. So love your Zairian parents and brothers who are counting on you to guarantee their freedom in peace. Respect also the strangers who are among us. This is what African hospitality and dignity requires."[87] Ultimately, Munzihirwa believed that every soldier should inspire "confidence and sympathy within us, instead of horror, indignation, and fear."[88]

By September 1996, the crisis was at a breaking point. The local population was exhausted, provisions in the camps were spent, and Western interest in the situation had waned. The Rwandan government was intent on disbanding the camps by force, and its military began training a group of Zairian Tutsis (known locally as Banyamulenge) for a joint offensive. "Anti-personnel or anti-tank mines are continually placed on trade routes in the vicinity of Bukavu and Goma," Munzihirwa reported in 1996. "The frequent explosion of these mines causes human devastation across South and North Kivu."[89] Soon fishermen on Lake Kivu came under regular fire, a

84. "Homily from Mass at Saio Military Camp," 140.
85. Editor's translation of Munzihirwa's original.
86. "Homily from Mass at Saio Military Camp," 139 (quoting *Gaudium et Spes* para. 79).
87. "Homily from Mass at Saio Military Camp," 140.
88. "Homily from Mass at Saio Military Camp," 141.
89. "South Kivu Is Attacked by Rwanda Today (October 11, 1996)," 177.

large Protestant-led hospital in Lemera was destroyed, and numerous civilians were killed, including two priests. A full-scale invasion was imminent.

In mid-October 1996, the armed group trained by Rwanda announced itself as the Alliance of Democratic Forces for the Liberation of Congo (known by its French acronym, AFDL). Led by the journeyman guerilla fighter Laurent Kabila, the AFDL launched what would become known as the First Congo War, lasting from October 1996 to May 1997. Alongside the Rwandan army (RPA), the AFDL began destroying refugee camps in North and South Kivu, forcing several hundred thousand refugees back to Rwanda. Meanwhile hundreds of thousands of other refugees fled further west.[90] Before long, the AFDL and RPA closed in on Bukavu.

FINAL DAYS

By this point most political authorities had abandoned Bukavu, leaving the city in the hands of a few remaining civil society leaders. As Zairian soldiers began looting the city, Munzihirwa urged residents to remain calm and support one another. "Let's come together and unite our hearts in cooperation to save our country. Today, as in the past, it is the unity of our hearts and actions that will save Bukavu."[91] He specifically urged residents to resist rising ethnic tensions. "We must be aware of the danger, of unjust and hostile intentions, and ward them off through prayer and dialogue. Let us never take it out on the innocent among us. We must say never to racism or genocidal intentions! Everyone is innocent until proven guilty. It is better to prevent war than to wage it."[92]

On October 27, Munzihirwa wrote his final letter, "Remain Strong in Love," in which he exhorted residents not to give in to false reports circulating around the city. Instead, he urged them to relay only reliable information and help foster an atmosphere of truth. He encouraged residents to remain in their homes, lest they come under attack while fleeing or expose their homes to looting. He appealed once more to the Zairian military: "I would like to remind these soldiers who are only strong in front of unarmed

---

90. Stearns reports that after the initial attacks in October/November 1996, "Half a million people returned home in just three days," but "anywhere between 400,000 and 600,000 refugees were fleeing into the jungles of the eastern Congo" (*Dancing in the Glory of Monsters*, 44).

91. "Open Letter (October 13, 1996)," 180.

92. "Open Letter," 181.

civilians to stop harassing us. Let them go to the front, where real soldiers belong."[93] He ended the letter with these words, "We Christians know that our greatest weapon is love towards everyone and prayer to Christ through our Lady of the Rosary. May the Virgin Mary, Queen of Peace and our Mother, intercede for us."[94]

On the morning of October twenty-ninth, Munzihirwa traveled to a convent in nearby Murhesa to rescue two Tutsi nuns who had been receiving threats from a local group of *Interahamwe*.[95] After he brought them back to the College Alfajiri in Bukavu, he proceeded to a local radio station to broadcast an update on the situation. Just before he went on the air, he told the host, "I am feeling my death; I feel it coming." Munzihirwa had a prepared text, but as he was about to read it, he put it on the table and briefed his audience unscripted. He spoke for several minutes, warning of the coming invasion and the likelihood of mass killings, ending again with an appeal for love and solidarity across differences.

Munzihirwa then went to a gathering of civil society leaders. When the meeting was over, he and his bodyguard, along with his driver, drove towards College Alfajiri via the Nyawera market near the city center, where they were stopped by AFDL/RPA soldiers. Munzihirwa got out of the car to speak with the soldiers, carrying his cross in his hands. When he identified himself to the soldiers, they asked him to sit on the side, while one of the soldiers made a call. The soldier ended the call, walked back over to Munzihirwa, raised his gun, and shot him. The soldiers left his body in the square, where it remained until the next day, when some Xaverian priests recovered it.[96] They laid his body to rest in a simple wooden coffin outside the cathedral, where Munzihirwa remains buried today.

Munzihirwa did not shy away from the subject of death in his writings. In "For a Christian, What Is Development?," he framed death in terms of a vocation:

> It is commonly said that those who die have been "called back" by God; death is effectively a vocation. We die alone because, to die, man advances to the extreme point of his individuality. No act is more personal. If the person must be defined in terms of

---

93. "Remain Strong in Love (October 27, 1996)," 186.
94. "Remain Strong in Love," 187.
95. Kyungu provides an extensive discussion of Munzihirwa's final days and the circumstances surrounding his assassination in *Liberté interieure comme fruit*, 164–75.
96. Communauté sacerdotale de l'Archevêché, "Veillee," in Cnockaert, *In Memoriam*, 11.

vocation, death constitutes the positive moment of his edification. Even if human separation seems to contradict the destiny of persons, it confirms it on a level higher than earthly communities. It proclaims, in its own way, the singularity of God's plan for each person, whom he knows by name.[97]

In his "Paschal Meditation," Munzihirwa returned to the theme, leaving us with words that poignantly, and presciently, capture the circumstances of his own death: "Despite the anguish and suffering, the Christian who is persecuted for the cause of justice finds spiritual peace in his profound and total commitment to God, in accord with the vocation which may lead him to death, with the desire and hope that his enemies will one day be converted to the love of all men. He dies therefore desiring and expecting human reconciliation."[98]

AFTERMATH AND LEGACY

Munzihirwa warned that a military solution to the refugee crisis would bring devastating consequences to the region. History has sadly borne him out. The AFDL quickly swept through the country, eventually taking the capital of Kinshasa in May 1997, sending Mobutu into exile, where he died of cancer a few months later. Laurent Kabila became the new president, and he promptly changed the name of the country to the Democratic Republic of Congo. Before long, Kabila fell out with his Rwandan benefactors, and in 1998, a second, much larger war began that eventually involved as many as seven African states and dozens of rebel and militia groups. An estimated 5.4 million people died from the conflict, making it the deadliest war since World War II.[99] Today, two decades after the war's formal end, large areas of eastern Congo remain insecure, with hundreds of thousands of Congolese continuing to live in internally displaced persons (IDP) camps.

Munzihirwa specifically warned that a military solution to the refugee crisis would result in mass killings of Hutu refugees. A 2010 UN Mapping Report documented scores of massacres committed by AFDL/RPA forces between 1996 to 1997. Page after page of the report describes refugees being hunted down in camps, forests, and fields, slaughtered and abandoned in mass graves. According to the report, "Every time they spotted a large

---

97. "For a Christian, What Is Development?," 33.
98. "Paschal Meditation," 88-89.
99. Coghlan et al., "Mortality in the Democratic Republic of Congo," 44–51.

group of refugees, the AFDL/APR soldiers fired indiscriminately at them with heavy and light weapons. They would then promise to help the survivors return to Rwanda. After herding them up under a variety of pretexts, they most often killed them with hammers or hoes. Those who tried to escape were shot dead."[100] Gérard Prunier notes that some 1.1 million refugees resided in Zaire in September 1996; approximately 834,000 repatriated, which means as many as 200,000 refugees likely died at the hands of these forces.[101]

Emmanuel Kataliko succeeded Munzihirwa as archbishop of Bukavu, following in his prophetic mold as an outspoken critic of military abuses committed against civilians. In his 1999 Christmas message, he directly invoked the memory of Munzihirwa, declaring, "We are engaged with courage, with a firm spirit and unshakable faith to be near all those who are oppressed, if necessary, with our own blood, as Monsignor Munzihirwa, the father and sisters of Kasika, Father Georges Kakuja, and so many other Christians have already done."[102] The occupying rebel force, the Rally for Congolese Democracy (RCD), eventually forced Kataliko into exile, where he died of medical complications that many attribute to the exhaustion of leading the opposition struggle. Today he is buried next to Munzihirwa outside the Cathedral of Our Lady of Peace. Munzihirwa and Kataliko are remembered locally simply as *"les deux,"* the two bishops who gave their lives championing the marginalized and excluded.

Today, the words of Munzihirwa fittingly live on in social media feeds and WhatsApp messages of a new generation of civil society leaders and activists who have claimed his peacebuilding legacy as their own. Among those influenced by Munzihirwa is Dr. Denis Mukwege, the gynecologist and Nobel Peace Prize award winner who rebuilt the Lemera hospital that Munzihirwa reported destroyed in 1996. The Panzi Hospital, as it is known now, is recognized around the world for its role in addressing gender-based violence and other health-related costs of war. In remarks on Munzihirwa in 2016, Mukwege observed, "Closer, much closer to us, right here at home, we all know Archbishop Munzihirwa. He took a stand. And all the counsel he used to give us, all he used to tell us in his homilies, we went through it, we witnessed it with our own eyes. We are living through that presently

---

100. United Nations Human Rights Office of the High Commissioner, *Report of the Mapping Exercise*, para. 229.

101. Prunier, *Africa's World War*, 148.

102. Kataliko, "Console, Console My People."

INTRODUCTION

. . . . [W]hen we cite Dietrich [Bonhoeffer] or Oscar Romero, those are individuals from far away, whom you could read as mere history. But this one is from here. He was our guardian."[103]

A beatification process is now underway to formally declare Munzihirwa a saint. At the time of writing, the process has passed the diocesan stage, and Munzihirwa currently bears the title Servant of God. On a recent visit to Congo, Pope Francis spoke to a gathering of bishops and reflected upon Munzihirwa's legacy:

> In situations of injustice and suffering, the Gospel demands that we raise our voices. We take a risk when we raise our voices in response to what God asks of us. One of your brothers did so, the Servant of God Archbishop Christophe Munzihirwa, a courageous shepherd and prophetic voice, who defended his people by offering his life. . . . [H]e was killed in a city square, yet the seeds he planted in this land, along with many others, will bear fruit.[104]

The writings that follow are just some of those seeds. May they continue to bear fruit.

---

103. Mukwege, "Role of the Church in the Pathway to Peace."

104. Francis, "Address of His Holiness Pope Francis." See also Allen, "Pope Extols 'Romero of Africa' as Role Model."

PART I

Development, Democracy, and Citizenship

For a Christian, What Is Development? (1985)

The fruit of happiness grows on the tree of work.

NTU PROVERB

THE QUESTION

SOME MAY DREAM OF a life free from the tensions and conflicts that accompany the struggle to find a place among the nations of the world. This is the happiness of a plant in the sun. We know it is a utopian dream: real happiness is born from struggle. It is not without sacrifice that human beings achieve the highest values of freedom and autonomy. Development is a struggle. But what kind?

Social development can be defined as a transformation of attitudes and structures in such a way as to allow individuals and groups to become agents of their nature and destiny; it is ultimately the result of a responsible, creative, and ongoing mobilization of resources and values aimed at promoting the individual and collective happiness of an ever improving society—that's to say, a society that is more productive, more just, and more united. According to Freud, in order to develop, one must move beyond the pleasure principle, or immediate gratification, to the reality principle, or delayed gratification, to face the complexity of life. By renouncing immediate gratification, one attains a more stable and enduring happiness. This renunciation is the beginning of progress and civilization. History teaches us that men of excellence always develop in societies where a certain striving reigns, which forces them to invest the best of themselves in the long term, often at great personal cost.

So the question arises: Is it better to be someone who achieves greatness through a life of sacrifice or someone who is happy merely living day-to-day? Is the perfectly happy man one who imagines he has captured eternity in an instant? Happy people, the saying goes, have no history. What kind of happiness do we want? That of a leaf in the sun, or someone who aspires to more?

HAPPINESS

To answer this question, we must examine what human happiness means for us, for man, for every man. Without getting into all of various traditional or modern ways happiness can be defined, it is helpful to consider the matter through a bright, revealing, and unavoidable light: the light of death. If death tells us that life is just a momentary inbreaking between two voids, then happiness is limited to this brief "passage," and the politics of development limited to an earthly horizon. If, however, death opens the way to a more fulfilling, everlasting life, happiness must be conceived according to an eternal perspective, and socio-political organizations should account for the thirst for the absolute which is at the heart of the human being.

Among the various aspects of life, dying is important because it is something for which we prepare our whole lives. The final silence is a word of great richness for those who know how to listen from within. "Death is like the moon," a proverb says; no one has ever seen its hidden face. It is just another face of life, the one we do not see.

Death always shocks us. We experience a sense of panic when we realize that someone who was just with us is no longer present. The death of a father or mother is especially overwhelming, making one feel as if nature has come undone. This is symbolized in the way we neglect our hair, clothes, or the appearance of our homes, making us dependent upon the care of others. But after an initial period of disorder, society steps in to neutralize this brutal rupture symbolically and socially. Mourning is organized to comfort the living more than soothe the dead. We adorn the coffin and remember the deceased's good deeds. Little by little, we transform him or her into a being who has accomplished their mission, a protective ancestor. Those most affected by this separation are surrounded with tender support so they can bear the absence of the deceased. Mourning is also an opportunity to solidify the bonds between family members, who must support one another and welcome any children who have been orphaned.

Our customs have never considered death an endpoint, a door to nothingness. On the contrary, during the funeral, we ask the deceased, whom we call *Nya'Kwigendera*, or the "one who is gone," not to forget those left behind. We speak of them in a somewhat ambiguous way, signifying that although they may have changed places, they remain close; we talk to them as if they maintain an invisible presence. The journey they make is only a mysterious change in being; their relationship with their family continues in another way. Funeral rites reveal a culture of participation in life. The happiness of the deceased seems to depend upon the rapport he or she maintains with the world of the living: those one left behind and those still to come. At the same time, the happiness of those who are on this earth is related to the life of those who are gone. This is a fundamental consideration that our development policies cannot neglect.

We can pursue this reflection further, going beyond the pessimism of narrow forms of traditional animism, and open ourselves to another wisdom, that of the gospel: only he who came from beyond to dwell among us knows the secret; he has transmitted it to us by his words and the filial attitude he displays in his life, death, and resurrection.

It is commonly said that those who die have been "called back" by God; death is effectively a vocation. We die alone because, to die, man advances to the extreme point of his individuality. No act is more personal. If the person must be defined in terms of vocation, death constitutes the positive moment of his edification. Even if human separation seems to contradict the destiny of persons, it confirms it on a level higher than earthly communities. It proclaims, in its own way, the singularity of God's plan for each person, whom he knows by name. The divine dialogue encompasses the earthly dialogue. God calls us in his love and everything else fades away. Here we come to the root of the respect that is due to every human being, the sacred element that must be taken into account in all socio-economic activity. What is true for a person is true for all human beings sustained by a loving creator. And here we enter into a brotherhood without limit, where the happiness of one is the happiness of all.

Jesus is the living way who guides and enlightens us; by his death and resurrection, he leads us to where he abides with the Father, which is neither a place nor a time, but a presence, the source of all newness. He acts in our life as an ever-renewing inner light, enabling us to live each day with a new heart. In virtue of his human steps, he is a traveler with us; in virtue of his resurrected nature, he is already at the end of the journey welcoming us.

If we are faithful to him, we can face life and death with hope. From now on, instead of living only to die, we die in order to live. Our existence passes from life to life.

FREEDOM

The light of death points us to the spiritual dimension of life; it points us to our relationship with others and our relationship with the wholly Other. It was this light which became dazzling in the death of the Prophet Jesus of Nazareth. Without leaving this behind, let us return to our question: what kind of happiness do we want to pursue through our development policies?

Pursuing happiness means taking charge, assuming responsibility for oneself. Is there a heavier burden? What individual, group, or nation has not at some point sought to relinquish this task? We think that if we were released from this burden, the road would be easier. When the soul is heavy and the body tired, there arises within each of us the temptation of pursuing a happiness devoid of any investment in the world around us, that is to say, a happiness found in escape.

Such escape basically surrenders control of one's mind and body to someone else, someone who will think for me and provide for me. It is easier to have someone think for us. This allows us simply to amuse ourselves, losing ourselves in a certain euphoria, and letting others worry about the future. When most people have their basic needs met, they are not interested in accepting the costs of freedom. Those who seek only games and entertainment, however, prepare themselves for slavery. A nation often achieves and sustains freedom thanks to the efforts of a select few, but servitude awaits those who succumb to the temptation of an easy happiness. In the story of the Grand Inquisitor from Dostoevsky's *Brothers Karamazov*, the central character accuses Jesus of being too demanding, requiring sacrifice in order to realize happiness. Pain is the daughter of freedom, and since it is happiness that humanity wants, [the Inquisitor reasons that] freedom must be repressed in order to eliminate pain.[1] Freedom is indeed heavy to bear because it is hard to bear oneself. But what respect does an individual or group deserve when they prefer such passive happiness to freedom?

What is freedom in a nation? It is not simply the capacity to make individual choices. It can be conceived as a balance between an individual

---

1. Lacroix, *Sens du dialogue*, 119–23. [All footnotes that follow are original except where indicated.]

feeling of autonomy and external constraint, that is to say, an accord between autonomy and certain communal values. This accord is only possible through a recognition of the rational and non-arbitrary nature of the constraint, its conformity to the demands of reason and human dignity, i.e., when a person feels that his or her activity contributes to the destiny of the wider community of the nation in the modern sense of the word. A nation, Renan writes, "is a soul, a spiritual principle of men living in the same territorial community . . . having common glories in the past and a will to continue them in the present."[2] In this sense, the nation is not an already constituted reality like a tribe, but a project. It is not a pre-established fact, but something constructed, or better, a *will* to construct. It is, therefore, not origin or common language that makes a nation, but the will to live together. And the strongest nations are those that have been able to forge a common soul out of its ethnic diversity, when, by a fair distribution of rights and duties, everyone feels represented, even when one is not on top. If one group has great responsibility in the nation, it is only because it has been delegated; otherwise, it has usurped that power and cut it off from its roots, weakening the nation, fomenting division, and perhaps opening the door to anarchy. This happens when an individual or group feels alienated and no longer finds their work or life aligns with the good of the community. This weakens the nation's sense of integral development.

STRUGGLE

No one questions the need for economic growth in order to overcome poverty. Still, there is little agreement over how development should proceed, or who should decide which areas ought to be prioritized. Opinions diverge depending upon what kind of society should be built, with some favoring an aristocratic or plutocratic society permitting significant inequality, and others supporting a democratic society rooted in egalitarianism. From an economic point of view, the first option benefits the rich; money flows directly to the wealthy and only indirectly to those in need; this leads us very far off the path of happiness that we should be seeking, the horizon of a shared humanity, now and beyond death. The second option seeks to give equal opportunity to all.

When development is debated in academic circles, two theses often clash. The first emphasizes self-reliance. On this view, all efforts must first

2. Renan, *Qu'est-ce qu'une nation?*, 26.

be directed towards meeting basic needs. Mobilizing the country's human and material resources takes priority. At the international level, the country must strengthen its economic, commercial, and monetary ties with its neighboring countries. Only then can it open itself to the international community more broadly. Proponents of the second thesis believe that, pressed for time, Africa must make the best possible use of the experience of industrialized countries, in particular, by intensifying international industrial cooperation.

Each option has its merits, but to succeed, one has to make difficult decisions about what to prioritize.

An economy is like a pot resting on three stones, each of which is necessary for it to remain in balance:

- raw materials extracted from nature;
- capital to equip and pay the work force;
- the brain power necessary for organizing the work.

At present, this last factor is more important than the others. Those who possess advanced technology have easier access to capital and raw materials.

The proponents of the first thesis propose compensating for the lack of capital through austerity and social organization. They should be the first to adopt the austerity they wish to impose upon others; they should practice modesty in their own consumption if they want their country to consume less than it produces. They must set the example. In order to educate a society of producers, the educators must themselves be educated and accountable to the people. This is what we call the dialogue between the rulers and the ruled. Tanzania seems to have made a start in this direction. But to bring about greater equality, how many others are willing to follow Mwalimu's example of austerity in order to reform the entire salary structure of the country? Nyerere set an example for his people: "modest revenue, a simple home, an old Land-Rover to travel the country; one observer noted it was as if the practice of the first Christians had been turned into an entire political economy."[3] Respected, loved, and appreciated by the people, Nyerere nonetheless had difficulty applying this philosophy to the party system. Certain influential members of Tanzanian politics adhered

---

3. Grand-Maison, "Tanzanie, un nouveau socialism africain?," 6. See also, by the same author, "Parti liberal de la Côte-d'Ivoire," 2–12.

to the commonly held belief in contemporary Africa that the party and the country are one. They presume the good of the country belongs to the party, even though the party is, by definition, only a part of the nation. The other difficulty with Nyerere's socialism stems from the fact that the traditional foundations of what he calls "African socialism" were shaken by colonialism and the international valorization of personal success as the driver of action. An African proverb says, "One is more a child of one's time than one's parents." This means that the child responds more to the ideas of his teachers and surrounding environment than those of his parents. The elite in contemporary Tanzania have been formed by the liberal, English bourgeoisie. It is difficult to accomplish socialism without any socialists. Let's credit Nyerere for giving an important boost to an alternative form of development. Tanzanians do not pretend to have achieved participatory, self-sufficient, socialist development, but they have begun a long transition towards it. They don't pretend that the *ujamaa* villages, the nuclei of rural development, are complete, but they see them starting to take shape. One can only hope that the stalemate and economic crisis following the war with Uganda will not undermine the promising beginning this fraternally minded democracy has made.

Liberal opinion on development, as informed by the second thesis, is clearly reflected in the example of Côte d'Ivoire. This country has opted for an original path between laissez-faire economics and a planned economy. It has experienced impressive economic growth. But the leaders haven't been able to "Ivoirize" this economy. This is because there are leaks everywhere; some partners thwart the diversification of international trade, to such an extent that one wonders if it is less an economic miracle than an economic mirage. One author has ironically declared, "This is a miracle that consists of a French brain and robotic arms," suggesting that Ivoirians want to get rich by doing nothing. This observation generalizes too much, and ignores the well-meaning attempt of citizens to build their own economy. It remains true, however, that many countries with an abundance of raw materials forget to consider the future and are content with immediate enrichment due to a favorable situation on the current world market. This is a dangerous illusion that causes one to veer off the true path to happiness.

Perhaps it is on two fronts, then, one internal and the other external, that we must wage our struggle. The proponents of the second thesis have to realize that their international partners are not altar boys and that nations are not the Sisters of Charity. The development of all people is a risk to the rich. Rich nations don't want risks. They want national security. They know that economic progress depends upon mastery of technology, but they prefer to keep at arm's length the countries with raw materials that would compete against them.

THE TRANSFER OF TECHNOLOGY

What can we expect from the much-vaunted North-South technology transfer? When we hear the word *technology*, we think of machines or sophisticated devices. Technology, however, is more than machines. It encompasses modes of thought and production in addition to technical equipment. To transfer technology means transferring the philosophy that undergirds it, training experts and technicians in how to use it, and implementing the necessary transformations to ensure success. A whole way of being is thus transferred, which will have the effect of uprooting the ruling elite because they are tied to a different cultural model.

Cooperation can be exploited and turned into a Trojan horse. This is what Susan George suggests when analyzing the causes of hunger in the Third World: "if it is true that we impose our ideas on the other half of humanity, then the question naturally arises: why do they allow it?"[4] Such submission is the result of a long-term strategy; the author cites a USAID representative who declared at the 1947 Coffin conference: "Our fundamental objective is political. The purpose of development is to maximize opportunities for private initiative, and to ensure that our investments abroad are well received."[5] We assume that this talk only represents the thinking of a certain group of capitalists focused upon their own interests, but this group is acting in the Third World. One of its methods has been to manufacture regimes that are outward-facing and designed to prevent the people themselves from being the true masters of their territory, and from having true leaders sharing their destiny. When, for example, tea, coffee, and cinchona grow in lands that formerly produced potatoes, manioc, and beans, we know the people will go hungry and the so-called proceeds will feed only a small fraction of the population.

Any autonomy thus depends upon our choice, and our perseverance. To be effective, our Christian commitment to integral development must be realistic and take into account this international struggle for existence, a

4. George, *Comment meurt l'autre moitié du monde*, 78.
5. George, *Comment meurt l'autre moitié du monde*, 80.

struggle for the true values of humanity, interconnection, and openness to the transcendent. We must believe that our efforts can bring about change. We must believe in ourselves. Christian hope, born from the memory of Christ crucified and resurrected, leads us to hope when there is no hope. It does not see the future of man and society with a naive optimism, sweetly dreaming of a possible future. On the contrary, it sees it with the acceptance of the struggle it will demand. It is an active and concrete utopia. It is only with great determination that we can expand the horizons of our underdeveloped region, which has, consciously or unconsciously, been trapped for too long by industrialized countries that have regarded it as a depot of raw materials completely at their disposal.

INDUSTRIES OR RESERVES?

There are some who take a wider view; they believe that if the countries that are reservoirs of raw materials themselves refined the resources of their soil, they would be richer and better clients. This reasoning, Alfred Sauvy remarks, "holds that the rich have other strings on their bow and should focus on selling finished goods. This happy solution, however, requires that the industrialized countries remain in front, and devote themselves to the latest technologies. If there was global equality in technical capacity, however—if, for example, Zaire refined its own copper, and Gabon its uranium—the richest nations would be those that had the most natural resources per capita."[6] If this were to happen, Europeans would have to emigrate to these richer countries in search of manual labor. This is certainly not what those who control the technology want. The inequality of the economic and structural forces currently playing out in the Third World is like a clay pot sitting next to an iron one. The two collide and only the former breaks apart. Moreover, one finds in the work of certain economic and development theorists a desire to keep the Third World in a state of subjection. Paddock defends the concept of an international division of labor, reviving the old myth of natural inequality, declaring that "we must recognize that most countries will never industrialize and that to help them industrialize would be a waste of time."[7]

Along the same lines, another author proposes that we approach some African nations, if not all of them, as "windows into a bygone era, when

6. Sauvy, *Fin des riches*, 273–79.
7. Sachs, *Pour une economie politique du development*, 290.

vast herds of animals covered the face of the earth. These countries could serve as retreat and recreation centers for casualties of the corrupt lifestyle practiced in the earth's industrialized regions. They could also have a role in promoting cultural diversity insofar as people who live there would finally have a way to preserve their traditional way of life. . . . We must find a way to help people accept the fruits of industrial society without trying to industrialize the whole world."[8] On this account, the development of the world proceeds at different levels. The old world and the "new" old world, the models whose highest values are currently in crisis, would take care of procuring the fruits of industry, and spare us the agony of development. But one can question the meaning of an ideology that seeks to approach the population explosion through simple biological means without nurturing any hope of economic well-being; in industrialized societies, it is the law of social capillarity that has imperceptibly reduced population growth without undermining cultural identity.[9] It is much the same with some pygmy peoples who do not disturb nature or seek to join any civilization. Again, what is the philosophy of so-called adaptive technology when it does not come from within, and its proponents do not have the patience to support the transition to the next technology? Perhaps they want to protect us from the technocratic alienation of an inefficient modernization, but only by relegating us to a past without a future. It is the dynamics of indigenous technology that must be carefully studied and promoted.

PERSPECTIVES

These opinions, which may not be generally held, are nonetheless more widespread than one might think, and show quite clearly what the Third World can expect from a "new economic order" vaguely expressed and advanced by some with a child-like optimism.

Nyerere's African socialism is attractive but weakened by the gnawing effects of liberal individualism. Houphouët's Ivoirian industrialization is spectacular but menaced by the illusions of the rich. International policies regarding the division of labor, the easing of the population burden, the idealization of isolated cultures, the dissemination and/or transfer of

---

8. Cited by Sachs, *Pour une economie politique du development*, 290.

9. Editor's note: Munzihirwa refers here to the theory of social capillarity associated with the work of Arsène Dumont. See Dalla Zuanna, "Social Mobility and Fertility," 441–64.

appropriate technologies all capture partial truths about man and international society, but are they grounded in the same love for life in its fullness? What happiness do they envision? And for whom?

A life rooted in true hope cannot be bound by particular policies or ideologies. We must be aware that our future will not be given to us but will be the fruit of hard work; we must expect it from ourselves and not others; and we must not allow our hope to be misled by those who have an interest in keeping things the way they are. We must unite with those who, in the North and South, believe the last word has not been spoken and that where there is a will, there will be a way through obstacles to reach the shore of the future. What a noble task for a Christian! It is not a matter of backing down from challenges and indulging in superficial talk about democracy but listening to our inner selves and the cries of our anguished hearts.

A materialist vision of life regards human development as something that ends in death. This is ultimately to see life as meaninglessness. There is a Greek saying that a living dog is better than a thousand dead heroes. For a Christian, however, this life prepares us for a better, fuller life. Through the free gift of God, our current life will be transformed into the next one. That life is already being born in this one. From this perspective, death is a new birth.

The hope that the resurrected Christ brings us is the hope of the personal, collective, and total liberation of man, but it demands individuals who are willing to pay the price: "For those who want to save their life will lose it, and those who lose their life for my sake will find it." It is such determination that opens new horizons thanks to the certain courageous individuals who have opted to invest their resources in the long term. This hope does not evade life's problems but fosters an existential unity. It situates every moment of life on another plane, constructing eternity from the present.

Horizons can seem forever receding. Each stage may require new departures. The point of arrival may remain indeterminate, even if it is the end that justifies the journey. If we are united in heart and mind to the One who died and was resurrected for us, who walks with us and before us, leading us to life everlasting, little stands in our way. He is our living horizon. Christian hope brings together and underpins human hopes in the same spirit, going beyond them in order to bring them to fulfillment.

Development for a Christian is a dynamic that promotes people rather than riches, human solidarity rather than solitary individuals. It regards human beings not as ephemeral creatures doomed to oblivion, but a multitude that participates in a web of unlimited relationships, in this life and the next, animated by the One who is, in essence, Relation and Love.

Building a Nation or Developing a Country? Towards the Promotion of the Zairian Nation (1987)

AT THE TIME OF independence, many wondered if the African continent carved up by colonial powers, which paid little attention to cultural or linguistic boundaries, could generate self-sustaining African nations within the same boundaries. Some Africans believed that it was necessary to return to pre-colonial ethnic and cultural boundaries. It is therefore important to examine the origins of the concept of the nation as well as its constituent elements. Is it birth? Is it territory? Is it language?

1. DEFINING THE NATION

Literally, a nation is a people that has been "born," that is to say, a people that has become aware of its shared destiny, each living for and with the other.

The nation is often confused with the state, the state with the people, the people with the population, and the nation and state with the government. The nation, like all social and historical phenomena, is subject to change and has a history. Throughout history, the word *nation* has been used to refer to many kinds of groups, some of whom have nothing to do with birth in the literal or figural sense.

[Hans] Kohn reports, for example, that during the Council of Constance in 1415 to 1418, voters were organized by "nation," with the German nation made up of delegates from all over Eastern Europe and the English nation from all over northern Europe, including Scandinavia. In this context, "nation" simply meant "a group that has one vote," hence the cardinals asked to vote as "five nations."[1]

The word *nation* is thus of recent coinage, employed by lawyers and philosophers as a technical term and more popularly by the people themselves. The concepts of city, society, and sovereignty have long been fixed; the notion of the state goes back to the ideas of the French jurists in the sixteenth century and the great German and Dutch thinkers of the seventeenth and eighteenth centuries. The concept of the nation was much slower coming. In many languages it is still not very common in its technical sense, and it continues to be taken as synonymous with the state. In French, the word *nation* still designates what it used to mean: "country." In diplomatic as well as ordinary speech, one still hears reference to "western countries," "African countries," etc.

Priests versed in canon law were among the first to study the meaning of the word. Luther was already addressing the people of the German nation he saw reflected in the church and broader society, even if it did not approach the level of the Roman Empire and its various subjects. The word later disappears, returning only with the revolutions of the eighteenth century. It was not used during the English revolution. The constitution of the English reaction referred to "subjects" and "region." It was only eighteenth-century philosophers who explicitly discussed the notion, even if not entirely clearly or adequately. Rousseau and the encyclopedists brought it to light: "all power comes from the people." It was the leaders of the French and American Revolutions who then advanced the meaning as we know it today. The concept of the nation finds its precise form after the 1789 Revolution. Sieyès wrote, "A political society can only be an assembly of associated individuals." We have here the principle that all sovereignty rests with the nation. The nation is a group of people politically united in will and practice.

To make this notion explicit, by nation we mean a materially and morally integrated human community, possessing a stable and permanent central power, clearly determined territorial borders, broad moral and cultural unity among its inhabitants, and a conscious adherence among members to the state and its laws. We hold that any nation must necessarily refer to a people, a territory, and government, all three being central to the definition of a nation.[2] There can be no nation without some kind

1. Kohn, *Idée du nationalism*.
2. Maus, "Nation," 7–68.

of social integration, that is to say, some attempt to transcend divisions of clan, tribe, kingdom, or feudal domain. Such an integrated society must be located within well-defined borders, exercise control over its markets, and exist relatively free from foreign influence. It is particularly sensitive to its national organization, the structures that safeguard unity and promote communal well-being. But it is not enough to focus upon these three basic components; a complete definition must also include a nation's economic dimensions. It must speak to its cultural, aesthetic, ethical, material, and linguistic features, as well as how it mobilizes a spirit, a will, and ongoing energy that motivates citizens to identify with it.[3]

In sum, an effective national community must have a shared worldview, not simply a broad cultural framework but a set of common values—values which promote integration and a general consensus among its members.

2. CHARACTERIZING THE STATE

For the nation to be something citizens voluntarily join and participate in, two essential conditions must be met:

- First, there must be some sense of the nation as a joint enterprise, one that is collaborative in spirit.
- And second, members of the nation must be able to identify with it, or be welcomed into it.

This common will establishes a political reality, and it may not necessarily coincide with a single nation. It could be multinational. The state is defined as a sovereign territory. It is much more abstract. It is what brings order, balance, relationships; in short, it is what allows all the groups existing within the nation to develop without clashing or compromising their unity. The state is a legal arrangement.

In its mature form, this is known as the rule of law. This phrase means, on the one hand, that the action of the state is subject to clear and enduring rules, and, on the other, that individuals can demand that these rules be honored, claiming their rights before independent judges when the state violates them. This requires that everyone be educated about them. Legislation that protects societal welfare and regulates the economy is only

---

3. Vergnaud, *Idée de la nationalité*, 15.

as effective as the effort citizens take to understand, use, and benefit from it. Otherwise it serves as a mere weapon in the hands of would-be demagogues and dictators.

The nation is essentially the incarnation of the "social body" while the state is the incarnation of the political: the social is horizontal, the political vertical. Accordingly, the social functions by way of consultation while the political relies upon subordination. We are on an equal plane within the nation, but subject to the state. Even in a constitutional democracy with national sovereignty, the inhabitants are at the same time citizens of the nation and subjects of the state.

This explains the difference between what me might call a "man of the nation," or nationalist, and a statesman:

- The nationalist channels the consciousness of the nation; he honors it through his actions and inspires a love for it in the hearts of his fellow citizens.
- The statesman is responsible for the commonweal; he is not so concerned about specifying overall goals as he is about the means to obtain them.

It appears that nations adopt the means of the state to effectively achieve and maintain their unity, including, sometimes, through the use of force. The state is generally a reality which presupposes a national entity. History provides examples, however, of states which precede nations. Some statesmen succeeded in gathering various groups into one nation. Bismarck, we can say, "made" the German nation; the king of France created the French nation. But even these examples confirm that the nation is the "primary foundation" that statesmen must serve; if this were not the case, statesmen would become colonizers; they would not have the good of the nation at heart.

The nation is at the service of the human person. Properly speaking, it is more cultural than political. It is at the same time a set of values embodied in the nation's history and a particular, enduring human community instantiated by these values. Education serves to introduce individuals to these values, so in a real sense, the nation is only realized through education. But conversely, education itself is not conceivable without an introduction to national culture. This is why the nation can be seen as essential to a sense of personal vocation.

3. FORCES OF NATIONAL INTEGRATION

Four factors seem especially conducive to the formation of a nation: territory, religion, language, and culture.

Territory

Territory is the most tangible element, exerting an obvious role in defining the nation. Just consider the names of Zaire, Benin, Nigeria—do they not immediately bring to mind a certain geography? Despite the existence of nations without territory (like the Jews before 1945 and the Armenians to this day), geographic boundaries, natural or artificial, tend to frame the life of most nations.

Borders raise problems: Morocco, Chad, and Somalia know these well. It is tempting to assume ethnic dynamics contribute the most to territorial definition. Ethnic unity can of course lead to integration, but it is not absolutely necessary to form a nation. Gobineau believed that populations with the same ethnic characteristics belonged to the same nation. The German Nazis seized upon this idea to equate nation with race. But no concept is subject to more dubious exploitation than race. Racist ideology has no scientific basis since there is no such thing as a pure race. Fustel de Coulanges, who disputes this link in relation to Alsace-Lorraine, wrote, "If nations corresponded to races, Belgium would be France, Portugal Spain, Holland Spain, Prussia ... the whole world would have to be remapped."[4]

Sociologists know well that if a society is characterized by ethnic diversity, it is essential that it find a way to live together. This condition was not met in Austria-Hungary before the First World War. In general, ethnicity, far from being a determining element of national unity, is often a product of living together. "France," Renan writes, "is Celtic, Iberian, and German. Germany is German, Celtic, and Slavic. The USA is an assembly of ethnicities."[5] Even the Swedes, who are generally considered to be unmixed representatives of the Nordic type, manifest such markedly different physical traits that only a minority actually possess features considered Nordic.[6]

---

4. Fustel de Coulanges, *L'Alsace*, 9.
5. Renan, *Qu'est-ce qu'une nation?*, 15.
6. See Retzius and Fürst, *Anthropologia Suecica*.

Religion

Religion has historically been a factor in national formation. The Jews would have disappeared long ago were it not for the beliefs and religious rituals of the Talmud, and no one can ignore the considerable influence of Islam in the development of Arab nations.

Religion has played an important role in cementing the English nation vis-à-vis other Catholic nations. It also played a role in Belgium's constitution, separating the Flemish (Catholics) from Dutch Protestants.

At the same time, there is a weakening of religious belief and observance in many Christian and Muslim countries today. Thus religion is exerting less influence upon nations, despite examples to the contrary, such as Iran under Khomeini.

Language

"*Lingua gentem facit*," the saying goes.

Language is a powerful and enduring unifying agent; it is a mirror into the nation's soul, as it enables each individual to relate to certain shared features of life. It is a common treasury of feelings and ideas. In a word, it is the glue that holds a nation's traditions and customs together. Kessel soberly observes that conquerors do not consider their victories complete until they have eliminated the language of the vanquished.

Language may facilitate unity, but it does not compel it; the United States broke away from England, even though they speak the same language. Latin America and Spain speak the same language but are not part of a single nation. Conversely, the Swiss speak three or four languages but make up a single nation.

Culture

Spiritual factors are perhaps the most crucial. A nation is not ultimately a function of whether everyone speaks the same language or belongs to the same ethnic group; it has to do with what a people has accomplished in the past and their desire to continue together in the future. None of the preceding conditions can generate or develop a nation without an engine, without a "will."

BUILDING A NATION OR DEVELOPING A COUNTRY?

In his celebrated 1882 address, "What is a nation?," Renan said, "A nation is a great solidarity constituted by the feeling of sacrifices made and those that one is still prepared to make. It presupposes a past but is reaffirmed in the present by a tangible fact: consent, the clearly expressed desire to continue a common life. A nation's existence is a daily plebiscite just as an individual's existence is a perpetual affirmation of life."[7] A nation is a "soul, a spiritual principle," a "will to live together." Without such a will, it is a simple ethnicity.

Not long ago, Israel, Vietnam, Algeria, and Guinea-Bissau seemed to illustrate Renan's definition. But this definition remains very limited. If the nation is a group of men who seek to live together in virtue of their feelings of solidarity, their common joys and sufferings, their shared memories and aspirations, and ultimately their sense of destiny, this feeling or will cannot exist without an environment, as a human soul cannot exist without a body. The body of the nation, its necessary infrastructure, is its common language, culture, economy, territory, history, etc.

Will alone does not suffice. To the will to live together one must add capacity. There must not only be a "will to live," but also a "power to live." And some conditions must exist for nationalities to become nations.

The first is that a nation-state (or a nation in the process of becoming a state) must possess sufficient capacity in government and administration.

Second, the population and territory must be large enough for independence to be real.

This is why we should not confuse a nation with a homeland. The latter concerns a heritage handed down to us by our ancestors: in the land, blood, language, dialect, customs, folklore—in a word, the culture that is tied to a territory and expressed through an ethnic group.

While a nation may resemble ethnic groups, it ultimately transcends them. It is not like a homeland, determined naturally and reflecting the surrounding environment, *but a will to construct*, or better, a will to reconstruct.

It is a will to reconstruct in the image of an exemplary model or archetype. But to reach its goal, a nation must be animated by a faith that goes beyond the ethnicity of all of its members, its individuals. Individuals must become conscious people. Far from denying the reality of ethnic groups or tribes, the nation is built upon them. It draws upon their virtues, character, reality, and especially their emotional strength.

---

7. Renan, *Qu'est-ce qu'une nation?*, 26.

In becoming a reality, a nation enables different ethnic groups to become a harmonious whole, a single country aiming towards a single goal.[8] This depends upon the philosophy which informs a people's approach to education and their ultimate sense of human fulfillment.

4. VARIOUS CONCEPTIONS

Our discussion would not be complete if we did not address the issues raised by various political ideologies in our current context. How one views the nation will necessarily reflect certain influences, whether they are liberal or Marxist, whether informed by Islam or a dominant culture.

1) *The liberal outlook*

In general, this views the nation as an extension or social counterpart of one's conception of the person. Liberal nations, which have exerted great influence in these matters, place the emphasis upon sovereignty:

- popular sovereignty rather than the sovereignty of the prince;
- national sovereignty, or political autonomy, in relation to other nations.

The prioritization of individual freedom means national self-interest becomes the primary norm for action. Democratic absolutism takes the place of the absolutism of the monarchy. The nation that no longer recognizes any other sources of authority other than the will of the people at the ballot box risks denying any dependence upon God or transcendent truth.

During the French Revolution, the nation expressed the desire for unity across social classes, which led to the overthrow of the king and the establishment of a representative assembly, at the same time that it suppressed or rejected other views of the revolution, resulting in the totalitarian imposition of unanimity. In the name of the nation, the Girondins were guillotined, and after that, the Communards were liquidated![9] Everyone wants to exterminate those they consider beyond the pale, forgetting that those on the other side will view them the same way. This is hardly the spirit of "freedom, equality, and fraternity;" rather, it is the fear of freedom, which in turn unleashes a wave of reprisals.

---

8. Senghor, *Nation et voie africaine du socialism*.
9. Chatelain and Tafani, *Qu'est-ce qui fait courir?*, 282.

The assertion of absolute national sovereignty also tears apart the broader human family, opening the way to the nationalism and imperialism of the strongest nations, who simply see others as raw materials to exploit. It is a reign of sharks, even if the methods have the appearance of law and order. It will take nations a long time to discover that the world can only survive through acceptance and dialogue across racial, cultural, and ideological differences.

2) *The Marxist attitude*

Marx was not interested in the nation as such. His attitude was more pragmatic; he was interested in what each nationalist movement revealed about their underlying views of progress in general and the working class in particular.

He believed the working class had to organize itself internationally in order to defend its interests. This is because Marx saw economic society itself in universal terms.

Communists are accused of destroying the nation, Marx said. But workers have no homeland. One cannot take something from them that they do not already possess:

> The nationality of the worker is neither French, nor English, nor German; it is *labor, free slavery, self-huckstering*. His government is neither French, nor English, nor German, it is *capital*. His native air is neither French, nor German, nor English, it is *factory air*. The land belonging to him is neither French, nor English, nor English, it lies a few feet *below the ground*.[10]

Marx thus takes up the old ideas of Tiberia Gracchus, who protested the fact that while the Romans were praised as masters of the world, the only thing they actually owned in Rome was the air they breathed. But Marx's ideas are one thing, Marxism in power is quite another.

Lenin, who created the first socialist state, had to come to terms with national reality. Far from proposing the abandonment of the nation, he proposed the idea of national self-determination. He wanted, first and foremost, to prevent national conflicts from dividing the Social Democratic Party of Russia, which was composed of many nationalities. He then

---

10. Karl Marx, cited in Chatelain and Tafani, *Qu'est-ce qui fait courir?* [Editor's note: the original source for the Marx quote is, "Draft of an Article on Friedrich List's book, *Das Nationale System der Politischen Oekonomie*."]

wanted to leverage the dynamic power of national liberation movements to seize state power and use it for the benefit of workers. This explains why the Bolshevik slogan was "the people's right to emancipation through self-determination," the main objective of which was to demonstrate to minority groups that Russian workers refused to bend to the chauvinism of the Russian bourgeoisie.

Lenin thus defended the principle of self-determination because this principle would then enable a free and voluntary fusion. But at the same time, he believed that socialism could only be realized through a centralized state. So we see a certain fluctuation in attitude.

After Lenin, his successor Stalin went all-in on the centralized state, which he realized through violence, basically saying that the national question demanded the suppression of economic, political, or cultural identities that he regarded as parochial. Freedom was thus sacrificed in the name of development. But the revolution never came, and the promised reward—development and equality for all—was never fulfilled. Instead, a totalitarian state devoured its citizens.

5. AFRICAN REALITIES

In terms of the actual formation of African nations, the role of colonialism was decisive. Mamadou Dia captures this well in his book *The African Nations and World Solidarity*:

> Willingly or unwillingly, colonization carries the germ of liberation, by virtue of the transformations that it involves, the changes it introduces in ideas, institutions, and mores, and the basic services it implants, indispensable for the activity of the colonial society, which is itself obliged to evolve from the traditional to the transitional stage. Let us not expect colonization to be more than it could possibly become, namely, an ethic. Let us agree to judge it by its results and we shall have to admit that, along with its ravages, colonization—any colonization—makes some favourable contributions.[11]

One thing it did was break up the old isolation of groups and encourage greater solidarity, more suited to development.

In his book *African Elites and Western Culture*, J. P. N'Diaye makes an interesting point in comparing young African nations to past European

11. Dia, *Nations africaines*, 3–4.

nations. One could say that in Africa, countries are forming nations, whereas in Europe, it was nations conquering territories. The concept of the nation is still new for many Africans, who continue to think within the framework of clan or tribe, even as they live in territorial units from which they benefit but for which they are not directly responsible. Citizens are not yet sufficiently conscious of themselves as historical actors in a rapidly evolving world in which they must carve out a place to match their aspirations.

PERSPECTIVES

To maintain itself and progress, a nation must do two things:

First, it must recover itself through a regular return to the past. A person without a memory does not know where he comes from and forgets what he has done, and thus has no foundation for the future. Our fathers, in the oral tradition, had designated storytellers who served as "living archives," recalling their past battles and alliances. "A people who forgets its past," a proverb says, "is condemned to repeat it without knowing it."

Following this, there must also be self-projection. This notion is very recent and seems to have arisen along with the notion of development. It involves, in the first place, a projection into the future, knowing that "tomorrow already begins today." This is what leads us, for example, to develop five- or ten-year plans for the promotion of justice in a given country. Without it, all of a nation's wealth goes to the rich, and the poor are marginalized and excluded from participation in the national economy. We cannot just talk about the future; we have to bring it about. In the second place, there is an investment in the human resources of tomorrow. The children are the future of a nation, and the brightest future belongs to those nations which develop strong systems of education and training. The nations that are the strongest today and leading the world are those which, a century ago, understood the importance of education and invested significantly in scientific research while others were content to profit from their colonies. It is often said that poor nations cannot pay for good education; but often they are poor because they have not invested seriously or judiciously in education. Without this effort, they are condemned to serve as guinea pigs for all manner of economic exploitation and domination.

The future is in the hands of God. No one can predict tomorrow's natural catastrophes nor, for that matter, the discoveries that will radically improve living conditions. But we know that certain nations are already prepared for adversity, having developed models that anticipate different possibilities. They do not enter the unknown regions of the future blindly; they are able to face most challenges. Other nations are completely vulnerable; their governments say to themselves: "the future only matters to those who will be there," but they risk not having any one there at all.

Every nation is a complex reality. In many ways they resemble a tribe, made of up diverse elements, united by the will of their members. In many African countries today, nations are still under construction, but they draw their fundamental values from these tribes; far from being frozen copies of colonial structures, they must actively discern what is positive from modernity. Nations are an amalgam of whole peoples, facing many challenges which each citizen has a responsibility to help face. A head of state once said, "There are citizens who claim to love their country but exploit it rather than serve it; then there are citizens who have assumed their place in the social fabric, and it is only they who can be great nation-builders."

A nation's leaders must ask themselves these fundamental questions: Where did we come from? Where are we going? What are we doing for our people?

Cultural Traditions and Socio-Economic Development (1989)

DOESN'T EVERYBODY WANT THE opportunity to develop and progress spiritually and economically? We all know it: there is no development without being true to oneself, that is to say, without maintaining a sense of continuity with one's deepest self. At the same time, this core self only has a future if it is moved by a new hope. To develop is to be rooted in a past which is not fixed; it is to be conscious of the future that one wants to achieve; and it is to act in concert with a dynamic society.

PAST, PRESENT, FUTURE

Whether at the individual or collective level, all progress depends upon a double mechanism, self-recovery and self-projection. Self-recovery is what enables us to grasp that which has already been—what has already been given to us, and what we have become—in order to incorporate this into a living actuality. On the other hand, self-projection is where the present opens into the future; starting from the present moment, we choose and determine the future by the way we anticipate what is not yet given. A people that does not have a plan runs around in circles, simply repeating the past. The Christian worldview is oriented towards the future; it is a vision of hope.

Traditional, authentically African life is today, like yesterday, steeped in ancestral and religious beliefs, as well as social and cultural elements from the past and present. Without careful reflection, it would be difficult to distinguish the religious from the profane. This complex reality can be confusing and lead some leaders toward totalitarian tendencies. To see both the elements of nature and social reality clearly, we must take a step back and distinguish different levels and aspects of the same entity. This frame of mind will promote more effective action and change. But we should also be careful to avoid the opposite danger; in social matters, distinguishing does not necessarily mean separation. True African *authenticité* will demand a spirit of analysis that carefully distinguishes areas or instances of the same reality; it will demand helping individuals and societies progress while maintaining the unity of an organic growth in which all domains are complementary.

PROFANE AND RELIGIOUS

In our society, like others, there are many obstacles that stand in the way of progress. I would like to single out one challenge that we currently face. It seems that when certain members of the Zairian intelligentsia speak of African *authenticité*, they are only referring to what comes from the past. And when they speak of the present, they oppose their outlook to the Christian one, stressing, for example, the secularity of public institutions as the only authentic way to pursue the common good. We hear talk of ancestral tradition and secularity. But what isn't being said?

We know that our ancestors were not Christians. The Christian life is a novelty in our society, as it has been in all the societies it has entered since the coming of Christ. Early on, when one spoke of "lay" and "clerical," a layperson simply meant one who is not a priest.

But after the French Revolution, the term *laïc* took on new meaning. It designated all of the tendencies that have gradually separated clergy from the laity in Western life, which made the laity more aware of their shared position and motivated them to claim their full sovereignty in the temporal affairs of society as well as the state, in the intellectual sphere as well as the political order, ultimately preparing them for a peaceful but determined takeover of all the positions formerly occupied by the clergy. Opponents of Christianity skillfully shaped public opinion by speaking of this merely as a "social movement" and "agnostic doctrine," so as not to arouse the suspicion of many Christians because "lay" was not, after all, opposed to "religion" but only to what is "clerical."

As a noun, the word *lay* simply means someone who is neither a member of the clergy nor a religious order. This is the vast majority of citizens. As an adjective, the same word can qualify a number of nouns without any strong implications: we speak of "lay clothing," a "lay function," a "lay context," or a "lay power," implying nothing more than that these are not related to the clergy. But it is easy to slip into another meaning that abruptly transforms the meaning of the word. Since the nineteenth century, we speak of a "secular idea," a "secular state," a "secular spirit," and a "secular school," meaning they do not involve a reference to revealed truth. To employ the word in this way may even entail a certain hostility toward a particular conception of reality. We are no longer born lay; we *become* secular.

Henceforth, several groups have advanced secularism as an ideology to convey different visions of the world, sometimes employing terminology inherited from Christianity. Some call themselves "Free Masons" or "*Rose-Croix*"; others engage in a form of Gnosticism, theosophy, anthroposophy, or Scientology. These groups promise to liberate man solely through knowledge or wisdom, without the intervention of any higher power.

To take our discussion further, let's look more closely at one of these groups, the *Rose-Croix*, who regard themselves as secular, but whose practices give the impression of an esoteric, mystical religious order. The Rosicrucian phenomenon has penetrated various dimensions of the intelligentsia in our country, as analyzed in a previous article in *Zaïre-Afrique* (1981, pp. 219–31). I want to examine it from a different angle, that is, how it relates to our traditions, with a view to the development of our country.

THE SECULAR MOVEMENT AND ITS RELATIONSHIP TO GOD

Let's try to situate ourselves in relation to this Rosicrucian movement, first with regard to our traditions. The *Rose-Croix* say they offer "pure wisdom," allowing each follower to practice the "religion of their heart"; those who feel drawn to this ideal believe that it can contribute to authentically African life. However, there is something left unsaid, which is the gradual reduction of the religious dimension of life to a matter of mastering knowledge (this is especially evident with respect to Christianity). If we do not pay attention to the difference between what is said and unsaid, we will gradually be infected by this like a virus, introduced in small doses, that will cause us to drift away from our traditions.

Other secular movements exist: they may differ greatly from the Rosicrucians, but most of them share a similar point in common, namely, their opposition, at least implicitly, to religion, especially Christianity. There are the Deists, for example, one of the branches of Free Masonry, who honor God as architect of the universe. There are the agnostics, such as those who subscribe to free thought and make man the measure of all things. There are the Communists. All of these groups share a certain anti-clericalism which is ultimately rooted in a rejection of the human relationship to God. Can we find in such movements the "self-recovery" that will enable us to progress?

We know that among the adherents of these secular movements, there are some who are leaders of single party systems. But how can freedom-loving men subscribe to these two discourses: one that protests against the authority of the Church, and another that defers to the authority of the party, to the point of letting it think for them? Human beings are not always consistent.

Long before them, Martin Luther, perhaps planting some seeds of secularism, rejected all authority in the Church except Scripture. Some of his non-believing followers wondered how such free thinking could reject the authority of the pope of Rome and not the authority of Scripture (the "paper pope," they called it). In the same vein, some disciples of the Reformation, such as Kant, went further, conceiving ethics in strictly human terms, through the "categorical imperative," in an effort to give us "man independent of God." It is true that Kant, aware that the human heart is divided, subsequently appealed to an anonymous, universal Legislator. He anticipated what Dostoevsky would later observe, "if God does not exist, everything is permitted; but if everything is permitted, then I would rather have God." Once such a breach is opened, it is difficult to pursue the common good.

Let us continue with our reflection and ask if, in the absence of complete self-recovery (for example, joining a secular movement), it would be possible to engage in the kind of "self-projection" necessary for the socio-economic development of our country. Consider legislation, public service, or school: Can one promote development in these areas in a strictly immanent sense, without a reference to God?

In principle, all legislation should be an instrument of progress, an implementation of the ideals of justice and solidarity for the benefit of all citizens. But how can one pursue any of these ideals if in our public discourse one cannot say the name of God? As one observer puts it, we replace the Good News with the petty news. Negative secularism relegates religion to the domain of the family and individual conscience; religion is kept out of the public realm and the political arena. One seeks to legislate in the name of the contingent, limited, and transitory. Man becomes the measure of man, in his contingency; the words *justice* and *solidarity* ring hollow.

If we reflect upon the importance of public goods or services, we naturally feel the need for some ethical reference, some sense of moral and professional conscience. But with the hypothesis of secularism without religion, what will ground this reference? Can we maintain morality in the public sector when money determines the law? Secularism is not inherently irreligious; again, to distinguish is not to separate. But in actual practice, we see unbridled conceptions of the state, rampant individualism, a desire for immediate profit and social advancement, all raised to the status of absolute morality. In the process, concern for the common good, and the will to promote socio-economic development, wanes.

And school? It is an institution of public interest, but secular movements refashion it in their ideological image; little by little, the school is disconnected from religion and disconnected from the family (the only permitted refuge for faith in God), tied only to public administration. It becomes a temple of knowledge, conceived in absolute terms, a diploma factory, a crucible of wisdom without any foundation. Admittedly, it would be an insult to the freedom of the conscience to impose a single religion upon any student, or favor membership in a particular sect; but it would also be immoral to teach from a point of view that rejects or is hostile to the very idea of God. A truly secular spirit would recognize that school, even the public school, is a place of education, promoting freedom and responsibility, concerned with holistic education, one that gives religious culture and the spiritual dimension of life their due. We cannot systematically oppose the conscience of the majority of the population. Nor should we confine "self-projection" within the limits of the temporal and profane, lest we fail to promote social development at all. In short, we cannot promote the happiness of man by mutilating him.

CHRISTIAN TRUTH AND THE DEVELOPMENT OF SOCIETY

Before Marx made the idea famous, a Protestant pastor in London observed that the religious practice of the ruling class is a kind of opiate of the masses, keeping them resigned to their misery.

True Christianity is an opiate for no one: not the people, the rich, or the intellectuals. On the contrary, it keeps us from sleeping, arousing and maintaining a perpetual dissatisfaction. It is a principle of ongoing openness to God's will for individuals, institutions, and societies bogged down in the surrounding materialism. Because it tirelessly demands truth, it summons individuals and institutions, every moment of every day, before the secret tribunal of conscience, where all witnesses are held accountable. Next to these demands, traditional or so-called revolutionary justice appears artificial, imposed in a way that stifles questions and thus its own project of *authenticité* and revolution.

What we must critique are those forms of so-called Christian spirituality common among many of the baptized elite which attempt to broker a compromise, at the level of laws, rules, and habits of mind, between the evangelical message, on the one hand, and the violence of the nationalist state and pursuit of business profit, on the other. Such a compromise comes at the expense of the poor and weak. There are times when a population is no longer willing to be duped. When we look at the history of the West, we see that civil and human rights have only been won through great struggle. The religious formation of conscience and the mystical shocks of holiness have played no small part in these gains. But it's important to note that these gains are not attributable to a conversion of elites. Western society has been called to account and brought to heel, in large part, by the poor, who have become more aware, more willing to resist, and more adept in their organization.

MAGICAL BEHAVIOR AND DEVELOPMENT

Nowadays we meet many people, whether leaders of the *Rose-Croix* or other self-styled prophets, who walk around quoting all sorts of writings, including verses from the Bible or Qur'an, claiming a kind of immediate magical potency. They expend all sorts of energy in prayer sessions, bodily or spiritual trances, chants, and other animations, promising healing. Can we call this a religious sense? I do not think so. Religious faith transpires between man and the Absolute and implies creative reciprocity. It involves a responsible person before a Creative Person, a Benevolent Freedom, and Supreme Responsibility. It is with loving steps that we approach him; it is with a kind of fraternal availability that we relate to him. God responds to the heart and not by compulsion. He is patient and more humane than men. He is sovereign Freedom, liberating and not terrorizing.

Superstition responds to a need for security and protection against the unknown. It paralyzes action and blinds the conscience. Certainly, science cannot definitively resolve the existence or non-existence of the Absolute, but it can recognize that religious faith can play a mediating role, freeing us from the limits of reason, while superstition only separates us from reason.

True faith binds man to God. Superstitious belief separates man from the Absolute. It sets man adrift in nature, and chains his mind to a ritualism of gesture that has a predictable and mechanical character, preventing him from ever ascending to the universal. This is what creates the kind of individuals who, despite their training, have become incapable of scientific research; they attribute everything to the claims of this or that sect, which attempt to sway people with overtures to this or that cosmic energy. Such individuals are no longer capable of independent thought, and cannot commit to a sustained effort to liberate society.

Superstition is a deviation from religious sentiment. Religious man is humble and open to receiving the goodness of God and his free, all-powerful will. By contrast, superstitious man looks to trap mysterious forces and use them for his own ends. It is a kind of science that dispenses with the research process and the patience that it demands. This kind of approach produces only illusion; it masks a cowardice that renounces the effort that liberation requires. The believer proceeds quite differently: while submitting himself totally to God, he works as if everything depended upon his action.

The pseudo-mystical practices tend to center man upon himself, whereas liberation is a collective effort. In fixating upon our own essence, we blind ourselves to the ties that bind us to our brothers. What truly matters is a person who serves their community and country. Man is part of the destiny of all.

CHANGING SOCIETY

People will do anything to survive, which is to say, they truly want to live.

But can they do so without leaders who, with courage and hope, try to penetrate the opacity and gravity of nature, knowing how to distinguish contingency from necessity, and nature from culture? Only in this way can we find a way out of the maze of the international economy.

One of our proverbs says that to disentangle a complicated knot, it is necessary first to sit with it and observe. To do otherwise is to be like a sorcerer at dawn: having symbolically transformed a complicated relationship at night, he thinks he will find a new and improved situation the following morning. But he wakes up only to find he has been dreaming.

Those who devote themselves to Eastern meditations seek an awareness between enlightenment and emptiness: enlightenment here meaning the perception of the emptiness from which everything arises and into which everything returns, the emptiness above and below all things. This state of consciousness, similar to a dream-like state, allows one to think without any attachments or impact upon social reality, like a cloud in the month of June which dissolves in the blue sky without dropping the shower that waters the soil and germinates new vegetation.

Looking back over history, we see that moments of great social liberation only arise when the human mind has been able to make a clear distinction between the human and the divine, between the natural and the historical. It is important to know that where there is a determined will, there is already the beginning of a path out of the ideological muddle that makes international society turn in circles. When we grant loans to help pay off previous debts, is the intention really to cut or just tighten the chain?

Those who put their hope in raw materials should realize that eventually the soil will be depleted and only the spirit can renew it. We will only have a clear awareness of the value of things when we start to sell the product of our own labor. We must rid ourselves of the predatory spirit of gathering what we have not sown, hunting what we have not raised, and cutting down what we have not planted. Let us not be content collecting precious stones that we do not cut or polish ourselves. When we do not replant, we do not transform, and we do not take part in history. To take part in history is to act towards a future we share with our fellow citizens.

As one of our proverbs says, a tribe which does not plant what is necessary for the future of its children does not have a soul. No people was created solely to feed others, only those who have been reduced to slavery. Man must see his life as a long journey. Some nations pursue research the fruit of which only future generations will enjoy. In the same way, true Christians live for the future, a future which also includes the resurrection.

Democracy: What Kind? What For? (1990)

THE WORD DEMOCRACY CIRCULATES today with a prestige and emotional charge that leads some to think it is a cure for all of society's ills.

Different forms of government, one young man tells me, are like medicine; to be effective they not only depend upon their inherent quality or the skill of those administering them, but also how well they align with the people.

Actually no, replies another, they are more like schools, channeling the energies of a people so they can realize their destiny; everything depends upon the quality of the teacher and the formation of the students.

Let us begin by observing that in any political system, the important thing is not who has the power, but in whose interest it is exercised. Is it exercised in the name of the people for the sake of the common good? Or is it exercised in its own name for one's own personal interests? Or perhaps some combination of both?

The Greek philosopher Aristotle analyzed several forms of government, from the rule of one person or group to the rule of the people.

He noted that, in general, a single ruler favors formal unity, but is soon overcome with such a fear of the people that he watches over them day and night: this kind of government leads to oppression and eventually degenerates into tyranny. Dionysius of Syracuse presents one example of this. He beheaded so many of his opponents (and those he suspected of being opponents) that he could not even contemplate cutting his hair without fear of someone beheading him. And before long, someone did.

As for government of the people, it seeks to promote the freedom of each person in the interest of all. But, as Aristotle noted, these interests may come into such conflict that anarchy ensues, leading the people to resort to a despot.

All types of government, he says, are more or less susceptible to vice; democracy, he concludes, is the least worst form of government because it is based upon what is most noble in man: liberty and equality before the law.

The human being is always an unfinished being; our ideas about the future propel us forward, and we can only govern ourselves according to the image we carry of the future. The quality of democracy will therefore depend upon the image that a people carries of itself, how it conceives its "democratic soul." This image varies not only according to the people but also the times. It is dynamic. A progressive education allows the people wisely and effectively to take destiny into its own hands.

The face that sub-Saharan Africa shows us in 1989 is one of societies dominated by single-party governments; it is not a question of dictatorship for the masses, but of presidents who dictate policies without discussion with the people. Those in power present this mode of government as "authentically African." However, upon closer inspection, today's regimes are neither a reflection nor a legacy of the kind of governance practiced by our ancestors.

The origin of today's African dictatorships goes back to the end of the nineteenth century, when colonizers from Western Europe established their dominion over our continent. At that time, the governors were sent by the metropoles; they did not feel responsible in any way for the people they ruled: it was a government of occupation that did not listen to them. While they may have occasionally collaborated with some indigenous groups, foreigners made the decisions that mattered. This type of power was based upon a simple assumption: Africans were not fit for democracy, much less independence.

After political independence, the same model was introduced almost everywhere in Africa by the men who took over from the colonial powers. As soon as they took power, African leaders rushed to abolish the constitutional laws that permitted freedom of speech, asserting that their people were not prepared for democracy, that a multi-party system was divisive and provoked ethnic hostility, and that class struggle did not exist in Africa.

DEMOCRACY: WHAT KIND? WHAT FOR?

Too many of us fell for this kind of justification, tricked into seeing ourselves as a unique people endowed with the enviable qualities of peace, love, and unity.

Accepting this image of ourselves, we allowed these leaders to assume the role of father-figures managing a common heritage for the good of all! Under this cover, social classes developed: those in power diverted public funds into their private accounts while their fellow citizens had no means to check it. Single-party rule hid internal tensions instead of bringing them to light. It gave rise to what sociologists call "kleptocracy," i.e., the creation of an economic situation where public funds are plundered at will. There was nothing democratic about this political struggle; it was just one big game of influence. The people did not have the means to identify where the abuses were coming from and who was responsible; they could not participate in the decisions that would reform the system and promote a politics that served the common good.

On the contrary, through terror, the Party-State installed the peace of the cemetery, draining the living energies of the nation and perpetuating a system of cheap labor and economic exploitation. Moreover, the system consolidated the interests of the indigenous leaders and, paradoxically, those of the multinationals. This is what is commonly called "neo-colonialism," or the combination of internal and external exploitation, carried out as if by an invisible hand. Multinationals thus claim that democracy is not African, and that this form of government is only suitable to economically and industrially developed countries. Some have even said that democracy is essentially European, tracing its origin to ancient Greece.

Is this really the case?

Is the origin of democracy so unique? Was ancient Greece more democratically organized than some of our African villages?

In ancient Greece, society was divided into two groups: the lower class, composed of slaves and various craftsmen, and the upper class, composed of leaders of society such as intellectuals and soldiers, citizens who were free from manual labor. The intellectuals had the leisure to philosophize in the *agora* and discuss the affairs of the city. The lower class may have been larger, but it was preoccupied with material production and did not have access to the political process. The ruling Greeks were proud to govern themselves by speech; they scorned the "barbarians" who only obeyed the strength of despots or tyrants—people who killed instead of debating. This was government by "discourse and reason," not force, part of what some call the "Greek miracle."

Can we say, however, there was more democracy in Greece than some of our African villages?

In the past, and in some places to this day, adults would meet every evening under the *baraza* to discuss village affairs; from time to time, they gathered for a day-long *palaver*. Such meetings could last a long time, until the discussion reached unanimity, or a broad consensus. According to the customs, those who did not agree with the decision would still accept it. This was a path to real democracy. It had its own characteristics. The principle of unanimity, which was fundamental, guaranteed peace even if it involved exerting some pressure on those involved. It brought into play a diversity of opinions, even if, at the end of the palaver, those whose thinking remained unchanged, or who may have even been right, might not carry the day.

This kind of government was only practical at the village level, or among small, scattered groups who exercised their own autonomy. When the population increased, or when, for the purpose of common defense, chieftaincies were created (bringing together several villages under a single, centralized government), important matters were brought before the chief who no longer consulted every adult, but only the wise elders who represented their respective clans. As the chieftaincy grew and it became more difficult to gather clan representatives in response to each emergency, the chief surrounded himself with a more or less permanent council, which dealt with day-to-day affairs. It sometimes happened that the council isolated the chief, creating a barrier between him and the people, which opened the door to despotism. The nineteenth century witnessed a number of empires in sub-Saharan Africa in which the conquering chief did in fact become a tyrant.

These are the forms of government that led colonial powers and casual observers to suggest that the absolute power of the chief was the political norm in Africa. They believed that apart from the oligarchies that reigned over large territories, there was only anarchy. But this was mistaken on two counts: tyranny is not the normal mode of government in traditional Africa, and the decentralized village system was not lawless, but a diffused system of rule.

In Africa today, as elsewhere, citizens aspire to participate in the shaping of their collective destiny, and the denial of this opportunity can only be seen as a political affliction. Totalitarian government is such an affliction.

A wise man once said that growing accustomed to a chronic disease hardly cures it. The medicine may be hard to find, but this does not mean one has to give up; with patience and perseverance, we can keep looking for it until we find it. But the longer the disease lasts, the harder it is to root it out, prolonging the evil.

It has been said that in society, "man is a remedy for man." In all places, once a large enough population is reached, we have seen kings and emperors claim absolute power. This situation lasts for centuries, but each time, people eventually rise up against absolutism and reclaim power. In the European Middle Ages, we saw the emergence of commercial cities which channeled the spirit of Athenian democracy at the local level. But it was not until the revolutions of the eighteenth century that we saw the establishment of the representative democracies as we know them today. Without question, this could have only happened when social and economic progress made widespread development possible. This political stage has not been reached everywhere, or in the same way. Liberal economies, for example, have excluded an entire mass of people from participating in the well-being and government of nations. In some countries, this exclusion favors the resurgence of despots, who, little by little, become dictators; in other places it takes the form of communism, which promise to establish popular democracy. This phenomenon, called the dictatorship of the proletariat, is now collapsing in Eastern Europe. It has become a disease that stifles what is most fundamental in the human being: the freedom to produce, within the realm of what is possible, what one wants and for whom one wants.

If human beings aspire to a democracy that promotes the development of freedom, and if they regard such freedom as integral to individual and social well-being, we must acknowledge that implementing it is not easy. Democracy has its own dangers.

Clan or family democracy seeks absolute security. But these systems can experience various social breakdowns, which have a sort of mysterious origin with no clear actors behind them. The practice of the *palaver* does not work against the invisible. Here the witchdoctor emerges, claiming the ability to expose hidden enemies, assuming absolute power and plunging society into fear. When these magical-political dynamics take hold, anyone can become a sorcerer or *ndoki*, some without knowing it. Those suspected of being a threat to the community will only find peace in exile. This is often how our villages end up falling apart. It is unfortunate. Certain expressions of creativity can only arise and flourish in a free society.

Representative democracy, which is more common in larger societies that have a modern state, is grounded in the principle of popular sovereignty, whereby the people serve as the source of power. The people give themselves laws and choose their leaders through elections. Thus those who hold office exercise a power that is delegated to them, which keeps them accountable to the people who are ultimately sovereign over them. But there are cases when people no longer obey their representatives, or when representatives seize all power for themselves, leaving a democracy without the people, which is meaningless.

The people must always be capable of checking the power of their representatives. This is difficult in increasingly complex societies, where practically speaking, the people only have the power to elect their leaders. In *The Spirit of the Laws*, Montesquieu observes that a despotic government does not need much moral integrity to maintain itself; the force of the laws and the prince's weapons substitute for this. By contrast, in a popular or democratic state, one must have an additional spring: virtue. Love of country, equality, the spirit of justice and fairness in the management of public affairs, the right to free speech granted to all—these are the elements of a true democracy. A democracy is a school of patience and mutual listening. When these conditions are not present, the people will either be trampled upon for the benefit of a few or rise up in revolution.

Some believe that when a situation becomes unbearable, revolution is the necessary path to a new beginning. Quickly replace the leaders, the thinking goes, and everything will be better! It is not so simple. One often ends up with something worse. A truly fruitful, creative revolution can only be accomplished by appealing to what is best in man and inspiring his righteous and generous passions. Otherwise, revolutionary movements atomize the population and achieve a false equality based upon fear. Can this really be called peace?

This is how most autocracies become totalitarian.

Absolute power has always tended to "divinize" itself. For this purpose, it utilizes the intellectual weapon of ideology. Ideology is presented as absolute knowledge, providing in principle the key to happiness and allowing one to determine at any moment which attitudes conform to the orthodox position. Placing itself at the service of this ideology, a government can claim the right to absolute power because it knows everything. It rules absolutely in order to force its subjects to recognize that reality does indeed accord with the ideology embodied by the man or group who purports to know and control it. It imposes its so-called truth in order to silence any approach that would shed a different light on events. It ultimately obscures the truth. Lying becomes the cynical and iniquitous instrument of totalitarian power, violently imposed at any price. In the final analysis, it is no longer the lie that serves violence by justifying it, but violence that serves the lie by making it necessary.

Totalitarian power is always afraid of those who say no. This is because it relies upon the belief of those it oppresses. As a political weapon, lying is most dangerous when the actors end up lying to themselves. "At birth," Solzhenitsyn observes, "violence acts openly and even takes pride in itself. But as soon as it gains strength and becomes firmly established, it begins to sense the air around it growing thinner; it can no longer exist without veiling itself in a mist of lies, without concealing itself behind the sugary words of falsehood. No longer does violence always and necessarily lunge straight for your throat; more often than not it demands of its subjects only that they pledge allegiance to lies, that they participate in falsehood."[1]

An African proverb says: Whoever lies in the evening in order to have supper will be tempted to lie in the morning to have lunch; what will he do for the next evening's meal? In the end, he will starve, because no one will believe him. Abraham Lincoln said something similar: "You can fool some of the people all the time, you can fool all of the people some of the time, but you cannot fool all the people all of the time." According to another proverb, if you deceive me once, it's your fault; twice, it's your fault; but three times, now, it's my fault.

True democracy entails providing ways to identify mistakes and expose fraud. This is what saves democracies from the effects of their worst judgments, and limits harm when trust has been misplaced. Mistakes are inevitable in a democracy, but democracy can facilitate individual and social growth when it does not repeat the same mistakes and strives to do better. This is the role that freedom of information, investigation, and verification play in arriving at justifiable opinions, benefiting society and enabling it to advance towards truth and solidarity with dignity.

---

1. Aleksandr Solzhenitsyn, "Nobel Lecture," English translation available in Ericson and Mahoney, *Solzhenitsyn Reader*, 526.

Péguy said, "The social revolution will be moral or it will not be a revolution." We cannot transform the social system without first reforming ourselves, stirring within ourselves a spiritual and moral awakening. This entails digging down to the personal, spiritual, and moral foundations of human life, renewing the spiritual and moral ideas that constituted, and continue to inspire, the life of the social group as such—in short, giving the group a new sense of purpose. To want to change a society without changing its view of the world is to invite change through violence. One finds dictatorship exactly where one wished to avoid it.

Everybody now declares that in a pluralist society, only a secular state can establish democracy. A monolithic vision of society, defined by one dominant religion or ideology, runs the risk of excluding minorities from participation in public affairs. This sentiment is surely right, provided that we understand the word *secular* in its negative sense, as the absence of any identification of the ruling power with a single religion or ideology.

But what should the principle of unity be? Unity implies a common set of values, imparting a sense of solidarity that is indispensable to national life. As the social consciousness of a people grows, respect for the rights and duties of every human qua human is crucial to establishing a basic level of unity.

We could also cite patriotism, a common history, and a common language or geography. All these elements are important but not ultimately critical. There has to be, above all, a common will-to-live-together. As Renan said: "We have done great things in the past together; we are ready to face the future together." Through a common, living hope, the future will unite us wherever the past does not.

It should be noted, however, that without some reference to the absolute, man's true meaning is threatened. History has repeatedly confirmed the insight of the philosopher Berdyaev: "Where God is not, man can no longer be. Wherever God cannot enter, man will soon depart."

A true reference to God makes man a being, a person free and responsible for his actions and his society, carrying within himself the living presence of the Father of all, the One who wills the good of friend and enemy alike. As a wise man said: "He who died on the cross forgiving his executioners would never send us to eliminate our adversaries."

Any civilization devoid of reference to the transcendent, any civilization in which morality is cast aside, knows nothing of grandeur or heroism. When man loses a sense of love for this world and the beyond, he gradually loses his sense of honor and dignity. Absolute anthropocentrism leads to the eternal tragedy of man. The Greeks learned this the hard way when they sought to make man the measure of all things. Which man? Socrates or his executioners?

How is it possible to create brothers without a common father?

Ideologies have always had the ambition of replacing religion. The notion of religion originally contained the double meaning of a relation to the transcendent and the binding together of a people.

In the revolutionary discourse of the eighteenth century, thinkers called for the desacralization of religion and the sacralization of human justice under the tutelage of a Supreme Being. Robespierre put it this way: "The French people are not attached to priests, superstition, or religious ceremonies; only to worship itself. It nourishes the idea of an incomprehensible power, the terror of crime, the support of virtue, to which it is pleased to render homages which are so many anathemas against injustice and the triumph of crime." According to him, the people themselves become gods. But because the people identify themselves with their representatives, only the representatives are divinized; it is they who wield the guillotine with impunity! And that is what actually happened.

Ideology is thus the corruption of religion. It demands an act of faith in the ideological leader. But this act of faith differs from that of religious faith. For a man of God, a thing "believed" cannot be at the same time, and in the same aspect, a thing "known." By contrast, the foundation of ideology is to claim knowledge where it has no ground; to know what is true or not, one must adhere to ideological discourse without any questioning. Opposed to anything that would suggest otherwise, totalitarian ideologues organize a kind of intellectual terrorism against religion, philosophy, and science. Consider what Solzhenitsyn teaches us: "He who does not distinguish, confounds; and he who confounds, deceives those who follow him."

We also know that the purpose of ideology is to replace the story or image that a group has of itself. Indeed, every human group relates to its origin through a founding story, which fosters a social bond and provides the "glue" to a people's collective consciousness. In the case of ideologies, this is no longer a pure representation, but a political justification, a legitimization of the social order, and an attempt to perpetuate itself.

It also serves the purpose of domination, concealing the contradictions between the political discourse and the societal practice. It disguises what some call "false consciousness"; that is, the leaders hide their interests (which are in fact their sole focus) and pretend that the ideology serves the base. The slogan of "liberty, equality, and fraternity" allowed the nineteenth-century bourgeoisie to exploit the masses openly; later, communist leaders exploited the people under their own slogan, "the dictatorship of the proletariat."

Only a clear commitment to equality, the desire for which burns in the heart of the human being, can create the kind of solidarity between citizens that makes democracy something that exists in reality, and not in words only.

So let us acknowledge this: democracy is not "given" but a struggle.

Based upon the foregoing discussion, how do we know when a political system is democratic or not? Without trying to be exhaustive or doctrinaire, the following points are intended to provide some guidance:

1. The people must hold ultimate power, through universal adult suffrage, with each citizen having a voice.
2. At least two major political parties must offer a choice of candidates and platforms in fair elections held at reasonable intervals.
3. The community must guarantee the civil liberties of all its members, especially freedom of speech, publication, and association, protection against arbitrary arrest, and the guarantee of fair trial in the event of imprisonment.
4. Public policy must be guided by the public interest; it should promote the social and economic well-being of all.
5. The State must strike a balance between effective leadership and accountability. Those in power must continually face an opposition in the legislature, and all citizens should have access to an independent legal system that guarantees equality.
6. It should be possible to reform any part of the government through clear and peaceful procedures.

Democracy protects the freedom of each person, while ensuring that this freedom does not interfere with the freedom of others. Moreover, considered in its positive dimension, political freedom consists of the possibility of acting for socially beneficial ends; one is free to think, express oneself, and act, while respecting the thoughts and opinions of others. This does not mean that a democratic citizen must agree with everyone, but it does mean having an attitude of basic respect, which one observer expressed in these terms: "I do not like your ideas, but I'm ready to fight against anyone who would keep you from thinking."

One of our African proverbs conveys a similar sentiment: "If you bring a stick to the chief in order to silence your rival, know that one day it might be used against you." To promote tolerance is to give error the time to be confronted by the light of truth.

Democracy is also concerned with a fair distribution of cultural and economic goods: promoting equal opportunity for young people, equal treatment under the same conditions for adults, recognizing differences, and taking into consideration our various gifts and talents.

Democracy, Lipson says, can be expressed in the form of a philosophical equation: democracy = freedom x equality. Democracy aspires to fraternity. It respects the dignity of citizens, especially the least of these. It fights against despotism and anarchy. As a wise person has said, it presents sides that can be criticized, not because it is the government of the best or the wisest, but because it is the wisest and best of all possible governments. It has learned the lesson of Lord Easton's adage: "All power corrupts, and absolute power corrupts absolutely." To allow for, and institutionally protect, an opposition, is to provide a safeguard for the security and freedom of a people because such opposition comes from a love of country and respect for its fundamental values. Undoubtedly, the sophistication of modern power prevents people from exercising the power that is theoretically theirs. But alerted by their representatives in parliament, they retain the possibility of renewing or withdrawing their support for those who govern, always preferring those who attempt to persuade with open communication and serious exchange before imposing a measure or law. Through this participation, the citizen is no longer a spectator, but a social actor. He or she achieves a sense of belonging. And doesn't being free ultimately entail a sense of being at home?

On the journey of democracy, we always come back to the inalienable values of freedom and equality.

Freedom is a fundamental aspect of human nature. To take it away, for whatever reason, is inhuman. It is a timeless and unconditional element. It is of incomparable worth. We can undoubtedly improve its conditions, but at every moment in the history of a society, it must be respected. One cannot pretend to promote freedom by treading it under foot: it is monstrous to establish slavery in order to teach human beings to live free.

However, it is important to realize that freedom, at both the individual and collective levels, entails a formative dimension. In many Christian countries, a long struggle for spiritual emancipation preceded the rise of democracy, which prepared them to struggle against all sorts of autocracies. When we ennoble the spirit, we deepen our recognition of the fundamental freedom of the human person. We saw this process culminate in the 1948 Universal Declaration of Human Rights.

True democracy entails moving towards greater freedom, and towards greater equality through freedom. This process involves all levels of society: it complements the freedom of autonomy, or the absence of physical or intellectual constraints, with the freedom of participation, the direct involvement of the governed in the exercise of power.

Based upon these values, the State truly becomes a "public thing," that is to say, a project for everyone, by everyone.

The Great Palaver We Call the National Conference (1991)

THIRTY YEARS AFTER INDEPENDENCE, why are the peoples of Africa demanding national conferences? It is because for more than a century, Africa has not been left alone. It is because of the loss of cultural identity and political agency. It is because the people have been dispossessed of their social integrity.

Colonization confiscated power from the traditional chiefs and put it in the hands of colonial managers who were more accountable to their parliaments back home than Africans here.

Independence has not changed the situation. African successors to the colonial powers were put in place according to processes determined elsewhere; once again, the people felt subjugated and treated like children. Elections resembled theatrical productions in which those who declared themselves candidates told citizens how to vote; if they did not fall in line, the police were sent to tell them they had no choice. Once again, the people were led down paths they did not choose, and it is understandable why they do not identify with leaders to whom they are forced to submit. When rulers manage these countries without them, they feel alienated. We see the same crisis across all institutions.

But a crisis, a wise man has said, is both a danger and an opportunity: the danger is that one is swallowed up or carried away; the opportunity is that we can come out of it better, if we learn from it.

There is now hope for social renewal that can propel us into the future, a new societal project in which power is transparent. But this power can no longer follow the pre-colonial model of extended families or small clan entities, wherein everyone knew one other and what they wanted. Nor can it follow the totalitarian model that stifles creativity.

Whenever a population reaches a certain level and expresses a diversity of interests, its mode of government will undergo change. A *paterfamilias*, for example, is replaced by political nobles appointed by a king, governing according to a new vision of law. Direct control by the people becomes more and more difficult. More skill and patience are required in the face of a growing diversity of opinions.[1] "The virtue of patience," one of our proverbs says, "has bitter roots, but delicious fruit." It is this same patience that we now need in order to fulfill ourselves.

THE SHIFT FROM SACRALIZED POWER TO DEMOCRATIC POWER

A Ballot in Hand. Why?

In examining our contemporary culture, we see that it is one of juxtaposition, not integration. A dual conception of public power shapes our collective psyche.

First, there is a traditional conception in which those who hold power are perceived to be part of a divine lineage; we see this dramatized through elaborate initiation rites that appeal to mysterious forces that convey a sense of both clarity and obscurity. The participants wear masks and claim their power comes from elsewhere, an emanation or reincarnation of those ancestors who were strong like a lion, leopard, elephant, or some other dreaded animal. Playing upon the symbolism of the savannah, they say they wield the power to make it rain or shine. In this way, their power appears necessary for agriculture and the overall well-being of the group or territory.

Throughout the traditional world, people accept power through this vague awareness of its origin. They know that power is necessary because it prevents internal chaos and protects the community from external enemies. They also know, as many proverbs attest, that in spite of all of this symbolism, power actually depends upon the people themselves. Thus when abuses of power become intolerable, the people resort to the same symbols to justify the violence that removes the unworthy sovereign. When the people utter the proverb "All the subjects are king, and without the people, the king is

---

1. It is useful to emphasize the difference between tolerance and permissiveness. A son who has done wrong will be forgiven on the condition that he renounces his deeds and repairs, as much as is possible, the wrongs he has caused his neighbors and society. [Note is original to text.]

nothing," they are saying that despite the threat of weapons, no one is above the people. They also want to warn the king that the power of symbolism and its effect upon the psyche notwithstanding, it is the people who are at the root of traditional power. The appeal to *authenticité* cannot ignore this.

Alongside this traditional conception of power, there is another, modern conception, which appeals to the rationality of elections in choosing leaders. This produces regimes that are either liberal or socialist. Both are often referred to as democracies: liberal democracy here, popular democracy there.

Whatever shape democracies take, the requirements of true democracy are everywhere the same, especially the respect for and promotion of everyone's basic freedoms. When they are not respected, the people take action and replace those in power. They reassert their own power and elect new representatives.

This demands the transparent exercise of power: that leaders conduct themselves in clearly visible ways. One can no longer hide behind mythical or real ancestors, behind the manipulation of sorcerers or ideologues. When something goes wrong, it is because of the leader's poor judgment, short-sightedness, or incompetence.

Even after they elect representatives, the people must remain the true source of power. They must ensure that power is exercised on their behalf. At each moment, they must be aware of how power is wielded and what it aims to achieve. The primary goals that democracy ought to pursue are, first, *liberty*, understood as the inherent right of every human being that enables each of us to realize our destiny; followed by *equality*, which, combined with solidarity, yields *fraternity*. This expresses and brings into harmony the love of self and love of others.

Such freedom, characterized by the absence of unjust constraint and by a feeling of relative physical and spiritual independence, can be defined as *freedom-autonomy*. To protect it against arbitrary power, individuals must participate in the functioning of government not only through the right to vote, but also through freedom of opinion, which requires true information: freedom of the press, which is not the freedom to write anything or sow confusion, but the duty to inform the people so as to promote the true values of freedom of association and assembly, which guarantees the autonomy of the governed.

In this way, democracy also serves as an instrument of justice that prevents freedom from becoming the prerogative of a few, as it was in the ancient

Greek cities which excluded the large numbers of slaves who were forced to produce basic necessities and supply free labor (hence the term *proletariat*).

Is our situation so different? In our merely "consenting" democracies, with their increasingly complex problems, the people rely on experts to solve them, without demanding accountability at each step. A living democracy requires such accountability, checking the power of those in control.

When the young have been trained to put more trust in broader social forces than their own personal strength, it is not clear that a democratic ethos can adequately take root, not at least without another approach to education. It is thus necessary for our Catholic schools to affirm unambiguously that while God may have created us without him, he does not want to save us without us. Our redemption entails a co-responsibility, and we cannot put our trust in a welfare state that promises access to freedom and equality without us. And it should be emphasized that the principles of freedom and equality do not go together if fraternity does not bind them together.

THE SHIFT TO PARLIAMENTARY DEMOCRACY

Traditional Power and the Council of Legitimacy

Many believe that the power of the customary monarchy was discretionary. On the contrary, if the monarchy did not permit a formal opposition, it had to submit to an elder council. One of our proverbs says, "The seemingly all-powerful king must submit to the counsel of the wise."

However, like everywhere else, one has to be strong to be heard. In some of the great monarchies, such as the one in Rwanda, the elder council, as keeper of the kingdom's secrets, was morally strong. When it told the aging king that it was time to give power to his son, the king knew what he had to do. And it was honorable for him to do what custom required of him.

It was the institution of the monarchy that held sway; a powerful monarch did not have to be charismatic. Sometimes it was a newborn son who was chosen. So the queen mother presided over the kingdom until her son came of age. In the meantime, the son listened to the elders who instructed him in the art of government. "A king who doesn't listen to the elders," another proverb says, "listens to the courtiers." But they only repeat what he says, or what they think he wants to hear. In the end, he only hears himself, like a madman talking to himself.

For us, the elder council was made up of the heads of the oldest families mixed with those of the reigning clan. They were called the "roots of the people." They were not particularly distinguished, but it was through them that the people deliberated and chose the sovereign. Thus, the people recognized themselves in this choice, and the elected official had an authority that came from the base.

The Value of the Ballot

It has become common to define democracy as government of the people, by the people, and for the people. This underscores the absolute sovereignty of the people. In Western democracy, the sovereign people decide through the ballot. This is what allows them to bring about social change. What can they change? In theory, everything, but in practice, often not much, because despite the ability to vote, a small class monopolizes power and the economy.

How is this possible? It is due to the centralization of the electoral system, which allows a wealthy group to fund propaganda so they can maintain their privileges. This means elections are less a choice for the people than a legitimation of a power structure that exists independent of them. It is just a consenting democracy. A true democracy should start from the grassroots, from individuals who are close to the people they represent and to whom they remain accountable.

This requires decentralization. As one wise person has put it, there is centralization when "a few people" decide "a lot," and decentralization when "many" decide "a little." There will be democracy when many people are able to participate consistently, at different levels, in decisions vital to the commonwealth.

It is by no means clear how to do this in a world where the problems have become so complex that the average person cannot follow them. A famous political scientist suggested that there would be true democracy only when each citizen would be capable of understanding such technicalities as why the currency devalued by 2 percent and not less! Be that as it may, it is up to the elected officials to return regularly to the base; if not, what does a universal vote mean if, on election day, it does not allow each citizen to feel personally responsible and a sense of solidarity with all those who have the vote? On this day, every voter is in principle helping to run the country. The least one can ask for is respect for the role of the voting booth as a guarantor of freedom.

The Economic Basis of Democracy

All political and social power has an economic basis that must be organized for the good of everyone. A wise man said that he would prefer a poor king in a rich country than a rich king in a poor country. What should we make of the contemporary situation in African countries? These countries are poor, and their leaders are often rich; these monarchs affirm they come from a line of traditional leaders who distribute their wealth. Today's leaders take the lion's share of the country's wealth. They justify their kleptocracy with an appeal to *authenticité*. It seems those who hold power simplify a problem that deserves far closer scrutiny. Without a doubt, the exercise of power in our context, as in other parts of the world, brings economic advantages that place those who exercise it above others, in the alleged interest of all. In a hunter-gather society, the chief reserved the choicest piece of meat for his family and guests. In such a situation, greed resulted in the loss of power. In centralized kingdoms, the kings received tributes in food and livestock; this gave them the leisure to tend only to political and judicial affairs, and maintain their court and militia, who protected them and delivered their messages. But when the king was greedy, he created a void around himself; he lost the power to defend the territory and the people would go to the neighboring chief. The strategy of a good king was to be generous and magnanimous. He did not keep the spoils of war for himself, but distributed them to his soldiers. In case of famine, the tribute was distributed among the needy.

Although this may have been a pre-industrial context, a transparent management of economic resources is always a sign of nobility of heart and respect for citizens. Moreover, in all the traditional accounts of political power, the king is depicted as a symbol of justice, of concern for the least of these, a living law and guarantor of the people's happiness. If natural disasters and famines repeatedly occurred, the people would naturally wonder if the king truly had the ancestors' blessing. All of this indicates to us that a modern power that wants to be authentic cannot be content merely to watch over the territory, but must commit to a fuller realization of justice, and promote economic policies that allow the people to provide for themselves and develop.

The people are the strength of the state. A wise man once said, "There is no greater strength or wealth than human beings." If all strength is measured in quantitative and qualitative terms, one must have an appreciation not just for productivity, but also the collective sharing that is indispensable to social justice.

PART II

The Christian Life

Meditation on the Anniversary of My Ordination (August 17, 1983)

But rejoice insofar as you participate in the sufferings of Christ, so that you may also be glad and shout for joy when his glory is revealed.

1 PETER 4:13[1]

Before my ordination,
I wanted this passage to guide my path.
For many years since I have asked
Christ to give me the grace
to keep this message close to my heart.

May the memory of his cross
remain in the depths of my being,
so that I may follow him with courage as a true companion,
without ever wavering from him,
until the day my earthly journey comes to an end.
In following Christ,
I hope to find rest in him. He is the true rest.

Today I ask myself where I am
in my walk.
I can see that as I get older, I am still at the beginning.
May God make me
someone who is still a beginner, even as I age;
is not God himself always new?

1. Editor's translation of Munzihirwa's original.

PART II | THE CHRISTIAN LIFE

May he sustain me
during this new stage of life;
may he give me his wisdom;
may he give me the gift of the spirit of discernment;
may I be more available and more generous;
may all that I have be his;
may my whole being be in the hands
of the Father of the morning and evening, the night and the dawn;
may he be the sole aim of my life,
    my only Hope!

Virgin Mary,
mother of Jesus and my mother,
you followed your son, you attended to his teaching
from his birth to adulthood;
and on the way of the cross,
at the foot of the cross, you stood to receive his last words.
The only one on earth to hope for the resurrection,
your heart was crucified with him;
participating in his sufferings,
you participate in the glory of his resurrection.

Take my small breath
—my life is getting weaker and weaker—
give it to Christ,
so that at the end of my earthly life
he can raise it in his unending glory
with all the brothers and sisters encountered along the way.

May I be there as I am, an old man,
always beginning, before a God
who is always new.

Paschal Meditation (undated)

Nafe ahinga, Nafuuke arharhama (Shi proverb)
The prospect of death does not prevent cultivation.
Resurrection hope inspires devotion.

1. For the struggle and recognition
of human dignity
in our country;
on the way with Christ
towards the cross,
with Mary, his mother,
accompanying her
on the way of the cross;
we keep vigil
at the cross,
receiving the last words.

To see him die for humanity and our sins;
to accompany him to the entrance of the tomb.
To return to the city with Joseph of Arimathea, John, Nicodemus,
as well as the holy women,
until Easter dawn.
To welcome the Risen One
who greets us with
his peace: "Peace be with you."
This peace is not static, but dynamic, moving.
The way is long and hard,
but, as the proverb says,

what hurts the traveler's feet
is not the length of the road,
but the pebbles in one's shoes.
Selfish desires are the pebbles in our hearts that inhibit
our spiritual journey.
Let the pilgrim remove those pebbles,
and his footsteps will quicken.

We have a companion
who knows the way well:
he is the Way.

2. Amid the plunder, poverty, and oppression
that swirl around us,
we must find internal peace in him,
in the hope that God
will not abandon us.
Let us walk with the Church:
"*Rhugenda banga burhali bola*," the Bashi say, which means:
to walk together
is not to vanquish all fear,
but to be stronger, surer, and more effective.
To walk well, the apostle Paul says,
"Bear one another's burdens" (Gal 6:2).
Isn't that the meaning of the Synod?
Our diocesan Synod?

3. The peace of the resurrection is the power
of the Church during its earthly journey,
before it experiences the celestial joy that
we can glimpse in hope.
True peace has its demands:
it cannot be an easy solution,
a resignation,
an inclination to avoid, at all costs,
the tensions
necessary to strengthening faith.

Jesus, the Prince of Peace,
refused such a peace.
He dared to declare:
> "Do not think
> that I have come
> to bring peace
> to the earth.
> I have not come
> to bring peace, but a sword" (Matt 10:34).

Jesus does not want to give peace
as the world gives it (John 14:27):
the peace that he gives remains a leaven, a hope,
and not a state of rest.
Always threatened and always in question,
peace here is a struggle,
and not something achieved.
But hope does not disappoint (Rom 5:5);
hope is not a prediction about what might happen,
but the certainty of God's faithfulness.
Christ has given us the example:
during the agony in Gethsemane,
he first asks his Father to take
the bitter cup from him, but he
quickly adds, "Yet, not my will
but yours be done."
This is trust and complete
surrender to the Father
and when he cries out to him on the cross,
"My God, my God, why have you
forsaken me?," he says, "My God,"
because he knows that he belongs essentially
to the Father and cannot be separated from him;
in this he enjoys the beatific peace.
But God does test his human nature;
the Son intimately takes on
our sins, and says to the Father,
in Saint Augustine's memorable paraphrase,

"I am them" (cf. John 17:21).
God has forgiven us through his only Son.

The distinction between Father and Son
contains the entire history
of humanity's conflict
with God.
In his agony Jesus
is caught between the anger
of God and the refusal
of the people who have rejected him; he is suspended
between the Judge
and his solidarity with
his brothers.
Yet, the division he feels
is not, from his perspective, separation:
what concerns the Father
he experiences on account of being God,
and what concerns the men he adopts,
—whom he also receives—he experiences on account of his humanity.
Beyond the violence which imperils
his unity with the Father
and his union with his brothers,
his two-fold fidelity brings him
face to face with
divine equality;
this allows men to be
recognized as sons by the Father
and as brothers by the Son.

Despite the anguish and suffering,
the Christian who is persecuted for the cause of
justice finds spiritual peace
in his profound and total commitment
to God, in accord with
the vocation which may lead him
to death, with the desire and hope
that his enemies will one day be converted

to the love of all men.
He dies therefore desiring
and expecting human reconciliation.
Christian peace does not lack
"tension," this is why
we remain
hopeful that God
will one day be all in all, that evil will be vanquished.
Even when it seems
that the horizon is no longer visible,
we walk all the same,
as the poet Machado writes,
> Wanderer,
> your footsteps are
> the road and nothing more;
> wanderer, there is no road,
> the road is made by walking.

Our guide is Christ,
before us, with us, and in front of us.
Take courage, soon we will sing
Alleluia, Christ our
Passover is risen.

4. Remain vigilant:
the alleluia in this life
is a song of mutual encouragement for pilgrims
to continue the journey.
Easter this year
is just one step in the journey towards the new Jerusalem.
Everyone walks in accordance with its demands.

The family,
as source and root of life,
fosters peace;
it is the place where the light of faith is kindled:
"It is the domestic church."
May Christian families
be truly united, with

the love of Christ solidifying their union.
A wise man once said, "When God
is no longer the common friend that
each person loves the most,
each friend ends up loving
himself the most."
Selfishness can only produce division,
preventing us from walking in the same direction.
But Christ dwells in a family
when its members are united in his name.
Christian marriage is one of these bonds.

Public power.
The nature of its authority extends, expands,
and protects that of the family;
its duty is to harmonize individual liberties.
The art of leading the city involves
allowing differences to coexist
and contribute to the good of all.
Some say that the police represent the conscience
of the average citizen. They are supposed to be the guardians of order,
but in authorizing plunder, the regime has in effect
made them guardians of disorder.

Yet, the Council emphasized the positive aspect of
military service, when performed in the service of justice:
"Those too who devote themselves to the military service
of their country should regard themselves as
the agents of security and freedom of peoples.
As long as they fulfill this role properly,
they are making a genuine contribution to the establishment
of peace" (*Gaudium et Spes* 79.5).

In defending one's country against attack,
one thereby defends the human dignity
of one's fellow citizens and ensures
that humanity does not become a jungle.

PASCHAL MEDITATION

With the cooperation of all living Christian communities,
we experience the human brotherhood that
unites love of self and love of neighbor.
It is nourished through personal and
communal prayer,
by the sharing of possessions, cultures, and
faith in Christ.

Let us go back to the essentials:
> The source of true spirituality
> is confidence in the future
> and a firm commitment to freedom,
> respecting the dignity of each and every person.
> Through all of this, the true Easter is being prepared.

The Cry of the Poor: On the Occasion of Lent (February 28, 1994)

The cry of the poor rises to God, but does not reach the ear of man.[1]

Dear beloved,

The season of Lent 1994 begins under particularly harsh conditions. Faced with so much injustice and violence committed against peaceful civilians, we are tempted to ask, "Why does God allow his children to be abused like this? Why don't the authors of this violence, who are also children of God, obey their father in heaven?" It is necessary to meditate upon the words of Saint Paul: "Do not be deceived; God is not mocked, for you reap whatever you sow" (Gal 6:7). We believe God will have the last word. But in considering our fate, we are tempted to lose heart and turn toward certain false prophets who assail us from all sides.

1. Some of these prophets are sincere, but others exploit religion. We know that a number of sects are paid to create confusion among Catholics. We have known for a long time that certain American groups have encouraged sects originating from America or Asia to distract people of the Third World and prevent them from pursuing a collective project of development grounded in their own context. The experience of the National Conference and the president's recent remarks have also taught us that the authorities of this country have introduced these types of people to the National Conference and continue to encourage them to undermine the growing majority that favors a new social project. When these sects speak of Jesus, pay attention. They may be leopards dressed in sheepskins. We may speak the

---

1. Editor's note: this quote come from Félicité Robert de Lamennais, *Words of a Believer* (1834). Lamennais was a nineteenth-century French Catholic priest and philosopher.

same words, but not the same language. Therefore, let us persevere in the faith so that one day the real Jesus may describe us as he did the apostles: "You are those who have stood by me in my trials" (Luke 22:28).

2. Indeed, it is in the trials that God truly knows his own; it is in the trials that we discover what someone is worth, whether he is faithful, holds on, and remains strong. It is also in the trials that the evil one comes to sow doubt in and around us concerning our relationship with God. You remember Job who, in his undeserved suffering, was tempted to lose faith in God. But he remained faithful to the will of God. He is a model of the conversion of heart and mind to a God who loves us, but whose mystery is beyond us. We cannot be his judges. Our understanding is limited, our horizon small, especially in times of suffering. Let us trust in the One who is the Way, the Life, and the Truth. Let us try to take on the feelings of his heart, he who, in Jesus, was despised but did not despise, who was oppressed by violence but did not oppress: he loved.

3. This Lent, let us be willing to participate in the trial of Christ. In the garden of Gethsemane, Jesus is struck by a fear that could have led him to doubt. He asks the Father to take the suffering from him. But he quickly adds, "Not my will, but yours." Before Pilate, Jesus truly applies nonviolence: the one who is judged and unjustly condemned does not rebel. He does not yield on his principles either. To stir each person to examine the evil within himself, he asks: "Why do you strike me?" But he makes no threat. He is condemned to death; he suffers the violence of the political authorities, but his heart remains full of love for his Father, for his fellow man, even his executioners. It is in this confrontation between good and evil that everyone carries out the purpose of God in some way. On the cross, Jesus prays for his executioners, "Father forgive them, for they know not what they do." He was willing to suffer all of this for us, saying to the Father, as Saint Augustine paraphrases, "I am them" (John 17:20–23). Such an attitude in the face of suffering and death is a challenge to us all.

4. Jesus was hanged between two criminals. They both heard his words. But one only looked out for himself, wanting to be saved in the bodily sense. So he mocked Jesus. But something struck a chord for the second one; he understood the attitude of Jesus and realized that while they suffered the same fate, they did not suffer it in the same way. Jesus was innocent. Dismas—the name of the one we now call "the good thief"—understood that he was a sinner and that Jesus was the Son of God. From this came the short but profound prayer: "Jesus, remember me in your kingdom." Jesus

responded immediately, "This very day we will be together in paradise." "Happy thief," exclaims Saint Augustine, "He stole other people's property, and now he stole heaven." He was the first to be beatified.

5. Let us participate in these sufferings of Christ with the Virgin Mary. She was near the cross to encourage her Son to complete his mission. She remains in the background so as not to attract attention to her compassion. In the calmness of her heart, she receives the seven words of Jesus on the cross. She and Saint John will transmit these words to the community of disciples. She embodies the kind of presence that Jesus sought from his disciples in the garden of Gethsemane. Despised with her Son, she did not despise; crushed with the pain of witnessing her Son martyred, she still had the courage to accept a new mission of love: "here is your son."

6. When Jesus is at the point of death, he struggles again with his Father: "My God, my God, why have you forsaken me?" But he also expresses his absolute trust and total abandon to his Father: "Into your hands, I commend my spirit." Immediately there is silence. Everybody leaves. Mary is there with some disciples. The Sabbath arrives. What happens? A quiet but courageous disciple offers a pleasant surprise. Without talking, he quickly takes action. He goes to find Pilate to obtain permission to bury Jesus. Then he offers the tomb that he had reserved for himself. This service consoled Mary's aching heart. Surrounded by hate, the tiny seed of love remains alive; it inspires us to render a concrete service wherever we are. The little seed will grow and never stop coming back to life, to this very day. Mary felt it. Mary wants us to feel it in these dark and difficult times.

7. Jesus is hastily buried by a handful of friends. For the disciples, this seemed to be the end of the story. But Mary, who knew that "the one she gave birth to was the Son of God," could not accept this. She hoped that the Power of the Father would not abandon his Son. But how?

She returns to keep watch. And there, at dawn on the third day, she receives the happy news: Jesus is alive. Let us watch with Mary from now on, and more intensely, from Good Friday to Easter dawn. Let us watch like her, with a heart that refuses to stop loving.

May God allow us to sing alleluia with our voices, our hearts, and our actions.

"With the Family, Everything Will Be Reborn": On the Year of the Family (1994)

A child is born,

the world will not end tomorrow.

—NTU PROVERB

YOU ASK ME HOW I see the future of Bukavu?
Who can tell? The future is in the hands of God. But looking at the collapse of our institutions, our infrastructure, and our cultural values, we believe the future calls us to a persistent "struggle" in hope. And in this struggle, each citizen, each Christian, must look for, and find, the solid basis upon which the future of society will gradually be built.

1. Viewed from the outside, Zaire is a country at peace. No one talks about it. Nothing appears to be happening. But in reality, seen from the inside, it is a jungle full of militias who terrorize the population and hold them hostage. In Bukavu, for example, the new military authorities recently declared that they seek to reestablish state authority. They say they intend to bring the population to its knees, yet the civilians have only acted peacefully. Armed men in uniform have become *agents provocateurs*, stirring growing insecurity in the area. Is there state authority when the state does not know how to build peace, that precious good that we in Bukavu, like everyone else, are trying to promote and maintain through harmony and mutual assistance?

We therefore cannot count on authorities of this type. We remember the looting, shootings, and murders in Nguba, Nyawere, Nyangezi. Today it is the looting of the clinic in Ciherano, the murder of the watchman at the

Athénée d'Ibanda,[1] the diocesan staff harassed on the climb to the ITFM,[2] etc. . . . The presence of the supposedly disciplined and well armed soldiers is constantly increasing. Why don't we see a corresponding increase in security and decrease in crime? Why instead do we see an increase in brutality and banditry?

2. The Second Republic has worked, perhaps in a semi-conscious way, to put the people to sleep, to numb their sense of personal and social responsibility. There has been a corresponding erosion of civic and moral values. It is undoubtedly here that we must concentrate our basic, nonviolent struggle. Our role today consists of forming consciences in the light of true Christian faith, of deepening the true values which are part of our national heritage. The task is not easy. Besides the burden of poverty, there is a desire in the highest places of the Republic to weaken the conscience, especially through the promotion of various sects, some of which are religious, and others fraudulent imposters. When welcoming members of the National Conference, the head of state himself stated what we already knew, namely, that the bishops of Zaire are more preoccupied politics than the sects that have infiltrated the Catholic Church to weaken its power. Our churches must therefore develop antibodies against these viruses that are spreading everywhere.

3. Faith and justice can only be preserved when they are deepened and spread. They are deepened when rooted in the basic structure of the family. This is where nature meets culture. This is where early formation takes place, influencing the whole life of a human person, and even social, economic, and political institutions. Under difficult conditions, the behavior of a person formed by a family will not be the same as that of a person formed in the street.

We are victims of soldiers, that is, men who wear a military uniform and have a weapon in hand: these men kill and steal. What is of value to them? What kind of conscience motivates them? How did they become like this? Are they not the product of the streets and drugs?

On the other hand, we all know of other adults or children who behave with respect and solidarity under difficult circumstances. When asked where this comes from, they say their family and the school they attended. In fact, where families are strong, stable, vibrant, and fulfill the mission

---

1. Editor's note: The Athénée d'Ibanda is a secondary school in Bukavu.

2. Editor's note: ITFM stands for Institut Technique Fundi Maendeleo, a technical school in Bukavu.

God entrusted to them, the nation is strong. Where the family has lost its way, the young are confused and run adrift. No drug will foster a revolution, as one politician has said.

We must be dedicated to the family in a fundamental way, as the United Nations aptly reminds us when it declared 1994 the year of the family, and as Pope John Paul II taught us in his recent "Letter to Families," an essential message for the contemporary world.

It is in the unity and constancy of a relationship with one's parents that a child discovers a human environment and way of living. Here everything is education, down to the simple family meal where you learn to pay attention to your brother and sister. Of course, many of our families are fragile, especially because of economic constraints. Just to maintain basic subsistence, fathers try to exercise two functions at the same time, and mothers "rally the markets." The couple comes home late at night, tired and overwhelmed; the mother prepares the meal and no one has the energy to be fully attentive to the children. It's the young who are deprived of this education—the words, gestures, smiles, attention, counsel, and shared activities—everything that, through the father and mother, gives the child a basic sense of civility. The children are materially nourished, but they are culturally famished, to the point that the language they speak is no longer the mother tongue, but a syncretic gibberish of the street: a sign of the state of the soul, this language is imbued with violence and cruelty. The father is the pillar of the home. His presence is essential. When a father is missing, the saying goes, the child also goes missing. This is because he is a guarantor of order, someone who instills respect for others, emotional balance, and a sense of authority which helps children grow by teaching them consistency and perseverance. It is in the family where we practice justice, sharing, tolerance, and respect for the common good. Where the family has not carried out its mission, the policeman becomes the only conscience of the citizen. But when the policeman becomes the important figure, the country sinks into fraud and eventually terror.

It is in the family that the citizen learns to exercise freedom in a positive way: interacting with a father who exercises authority with love, a mother who serves with tenderness and without calculation, with brothers and sisters who are compassionate peers. We should not be surprised to find that politicians who exercise public authority with wisdom and professionalism had parents who were committed and loving educators: *the tree which we call virtue has bitter roots but delicious fruit.* The states which want to develop must listen to their families and seek to sustain and extend their authority.

Do we grasp that in thirty-seven African countries, youth between the ages six to seventeen represent 191,607,000 of the total 568,609,350 of the population (33.7 percent)? The world of tomorrow is the family's responsibility. It is up to us whether the next generation becomes a force of change or conformity.

4. And our schools? They are the necessary complement to the formation of the citizen, provided they are "educational settings," permitting young people to live together without discrimination of any kind, broadening their sense of belonging beyond the family to a social community, a homeland—the land of the fathers, or as we say here, the land acquired and defended by the arrows of the ancestors—and the surrounding nation which permits all ethnic groups to live together. The school must also be the place where various responsibilities converge, first and foremost those of parents, and then those of school educators; these are the responsible men and women who will train the men and women of tomorrow. In Bukavu, as elsewhere in Zaire, many parents courageously assume such responsibilities, alongside school administrators and teachers. It is a marvelous sign of hope.

5. The family is the key to our rebirth. It extends into the school. But it needs the right conditions. Many questions are worth considering in this regard, for example: *Should we defend a monolithic nation-state, or promote a national community of federated homelands?*

After what we have been through, "unity" has enabled the internal plundering of a state where no one really feels responsible for life or its goods. Excessively centralized unity leads to dictatorship, which ends up enslaving everyone, allowing those in power to serve themselves instead of creating a space of freedom and peace for all. It allows individuals to live merely side by side, instead of promoting a spirit of responsibility, complementarity, and tolerance. Perhaps the state-community of autonomous homelands could restore to citizens, and their families, schools, and intermediary bodies, their real responsibilities and rights. Ultimately, it is the federation, despite the difficulties that would need to be addressed to bring it about, that would constitute a space where everyone is taught to be "*for others*," rather than just "*next to others.*"

A conscience trained in personal and social responsibility by the family can help foster a state that truly is a public thing—a Republic—where everyone feels involved and can promote their own destiny, where each person can open his or her heart to international dimensions, to eternal dimensions, by learning tolerance and forgiveness of the enemy. Isn't today's enemy yesterday's brother? And therefore tomorrow's brother?

In Christ, everything is reborn. Through the family, listening to Christ, Bukavu (and Zaire) will be reborn.

Homily from Installation as Archbishop of Bukavu (June 26, 1994)

WE HAVE ALL HEARD this passage from the Gospel,[1] which describes the way in which Christ, before instituting the Eucharist, washed his disciples' feet. Later he said to them: "You call me Teacher and the Lord—and you are right, for this is what I am. So if I, your Lord and Teacher, have washed your feet, you also ought to wash one another's feet." In other words, whoever wants to be great in my Church must first be a servant of his brothers.

Today I stand before you, a Christian among you and with you. Every day we must listen to the Word of God.

It is often said that being a bishop means having power. This is not true. As Christ said, being a bishop is not a power but a service. And if there can only be one, it must be service.

Dear brothers, I ask you: In the family, who is the leader? The one who serves? Maybe you think of it this way. But in the family, who are you actually serving day and night? The newborn, the baby. The father and mother are completely at his or her service. In fact, the greatness of the father and mother lies in the service they render to their children.

In the same way, the power of the bishop, or the priest, can only be evaluated in terms of the service he provides. It is by the measure of their service that they will be rewarded by the Good Lord. The bishop is not a servant because he wears a miter and carries a crosier, but because he actually serves, like a father and mother within the family.

May those who claim to be servants witness to this by their good examples. We have several Christian examples to follow. On the occasion of the last Synod of African Bishops in Rome, the Holy Father beatified three individuals. One you know well, Isidore Bakanja, a young Christian,

---

1. Editor's note: Munzihirwa is referring to John 13:1–20.

persecuted for daring to profess his faith.[2] When he refused to throw away his scapular, he was viciously beaten and suffered fatal injuries. Thus he died professing his faith.

The other two were Italian mothers. One of them was named Elisabetta.[3] Intelligent and beautiful, she married a difficult man. It seems she never experienced a moment of happiness in her family. Her parents asked her to leave her husband. Her answer was categorical: "I committed to love him for better or worse, before God and his Church. I do not know joy; I accept all possible hardship for the sake of my family and especially my husband whom God may yet convert." She lived this way all her life, which amazed people around her. Her service to the poor only increased their admiration of her. She not only became a counselor to many people, but also led a life of evangelical witness.

After Elisabetta's death, her husband discovered, through her secret notes, that she had humbly accepted hardship for his salvation. Later, he converted, became a religious, and received the sacrament of Holy Orders. In this way, Elisabetta's prayer was answered. Let it be an example for other mothers!

The other one was named Gianna.[4] She was also very intelligent. She pursued her studies with excellent grades until she obtained her degree in internal medicine and surgery. She was devoted to the cause of the sick, especially the poorest among them. She had a heart for mothers and children and created a pediatric center for them.

During her marriage, she had three children. While waiting for the fourth, her medical colleagues diagnosed her with uterine cancer. She realized she was in great danger. Yet she insisted that her child be saved, even at the risk of her life. She died while her daughter survived. Her daughter, currently a mother of two children, was in Rome on April 24, 1994, on the occasion of her venerable mother's beatification ceremony. The Holy Father warmly embraced her, saying: "Here is the fruit of your mother's love!" Gianna's husband is still living. At the age of seventy, he was also present on the occasion. He was very happy, saying: "Gianna, when you died, I was

---

2. Editor's note: Isidore Bakanja was a Congolese man born in Bokendela in 1887. Munzihirwa describes the circumstances of his death, which occurred on August 15, 1909. This day is now commemorated as his feast day.

3. Editor's note: Munzihirwa is referring to Elisabetta Canori Mora (1774–1825), an Italian woman who was a member of the Secular Trinitarians. Her feast day is February 4.

4. Editor's note: This is Gianna Beretta Molla (1922–62), an Italian pediatrician. Her feast day is April 28.

very sad. Today I am filled with joy because you are in heaven. And it is you who will welcome me."

We can therefore affirm that Isidore Bakanja and the two Italian mothers listened to and put into practice the Word of God. They made it the pillar of their life. Can we not do the same?

Listening to the gospel is not an easy thing. It is not simply a matter of faithfully reciting verses, but putting them into practice.

I could give you yet another example. It involves a Zairian citizen, married, and a father of six children. His wife fell ill. She became paralyzed and was treated several times, even in Europe, without success. Despite the quality of the care she received, she became weaker every day. It was a real ordeal for her husband, Charles, who not only took care of her during her illness, but also looked after the house and tended the children.

Charles's family ended up telling him to abandon his wife and marry someone else since he was still young and rich. It did not take him long to reply: "If I had been very sick like her and she had taken care of me, would you have asked her to abandon me and go and find another husband?"

Charles understood the meaning of love and marriage well; in short, he got married "for better or worse."

My fellow priests and bishops, are we not supposed to be an example of Christ, putting ourselves entirely at the service of his people?

Being a bishop means being a watchman, night and day. The watchman's task is to warn when a thief or enemy arrives. Like the watchman, the bishop listens. He watches and surveys. He is always on alert. He must keep the brigands, the sowers of discord, the "wolves" dressed in sheep's clothing, from entering and harming his flock.

Do not be surprised that the bishop, like a watchman, is committed to his work, to the duty of his office. He is required to do so.

I would also like to address what is happening in Rwanda. We are scandalized by the inhumane treatment that our brothers are suffering. Unfortunately this is not new. Many people do not hesitate to shed the blood of their brothers in order to gain power or seek revenge. Can we speak of democratic power in this case? Not at all. The regime in power serves its own interests. The people have never found dictatorial forms of government work in their favor.

And here we must proceed cautiously. We must act so that the events in Rwanda do not happen in Zaire.

HOMILY FROM INSTALLATION AS ARCHBISHOP OF BUKAVU

Now I address you, our military brothers. Listen to me well. Your job is to ensure and safeguard peace. The weapons you wield are meant to ensure our safety. Sometimes this entails paying with your life! We are grateful to you.

More than ever, we expect real protection from you. May a citizen in danger find refuge and security in you! This means ending the extortion, harassment, and torture of all kinds.

I was happy to see the spontaneous welcome you extended to our Rwandan brothers and sisters, refugees here among us. They did the same in 1967 when Jean Schramme's mercenaries invaded the city of Bukavu.[5] What we do today is in fact an expression of gratitude and love.

To conclude, I invite all of you to live united as one. Let us avoid isolating ourselves by ethnicity, tribe, region, or hill, since we are all brothers of Christ, all children of God.

---

5. Editor's note: Jean Schramme was a Belgian mercenary who occupied Bukavu from August to October 1967.

Christmas: A Challenge to Human Plans (1994)

Unto us a child is born,
Unto us a son is given.

The Christmas event is a challenge,
confounding
both common sense
and human power.

God watches over human history;
our projects,
seemingly under our control,
come to serve
providential ends.

Pharaoh enslaved the people of God.
Unbeknownst to him,
God used Pharaoh
to prepare Moses for his mission.

With pride Caesar-Augustus
rejoiced in anticipation
of knowing the number of his subjects;
God used this census
so the Messiah could be born in Bethlehem.

CHRISTMAS: A CHALLENGE TO HUMAN PLANS

The twists and turns of history . . .
It is God who is in charge.

Curiously, the key events
do not catch the eye or attention of men.

The basket of Moses
which floats on the waters of the Nile,
and the manger in the Bethlehem stable,
are seemingly insignificant details.

God starts his great works modestly,
with no *coup d'état* or referendum . . .
The basket in the Nile bore the first mediator
between God and his people.
The manger in Bethlehem became the basket of the Church,
awaiting the Kingdom of perfect peace.

God does not shatter anything when he comes . . .

But why is Herod worried
when he learns of the birth of this little one?
The king uses all means
to try to eliminate him: he kills
all the children in Bethlehem under the age of two . . .
But Jesus escaped.

A wise man said: "Let us pay more attention to the sound
of sorghum growing than the trees that are falling."

The Son of God enters our world
where no one, or nearly no one, expected him:
in a lost place,
in a poor and unknown family,
in a setting of little importance . . .
at a time when his nation was colonized by the Romans.

His coming was unexpected,
despite all the prophetic preparations.
Popular opinion was confused,
because it was waiting
for a familiar Messiah figure, like Cyrus,
the conqueror who, in surprising fashion,
allowed the Jews to rebuild the Temple.
From then on, Jewish opinion expected him
to fit the mold of the "Chosen of the Lord":
an adult who would suddenly appear
with great fanfare.

Now here is a child,
who breaks into the world,
without noise or ostentation.

All of this is full of significance for us.

This year, the feast of Christmas,
is not just a commemoration of the past;
it makes us aware that God
is the one who is always coming into this world,
in fragility, humility, and modesty.

But where precisely is God born?
At the first Christmas, in a stable, a humble and hidden place;
today, in our hearts and families.
Christ is always born where we least expect him.

The joy of Christmas is therefore no light matter;
it is serious and grave,
because the shadow of the cross is already cast over the manger.
And it will not stop expanding
until the day when the political leaders
crucify, as a vulgar agitator,
the only begotten Son of God,
who came into the world to save it.

CHRISTMAS: A CHALLENGE TO HUMAN PLANS

Thus the Mass,
where the Lord's death is renewed,
reminds us, in the midst of Christmas, of the painful destiny
of the One who accepted humiliation
in order to raise man from his fall.

May the Virgin Mary obtain from her Son
the grace for us to accept the mystery of his birth!

Later, in order to eliminate him for sure,
the Pharisees did not hesitate
to have him killed on a cross,
and then monitor his tomb!
But the Lord is resurrected:
this is his definitive birth.

In Rome, Nero also
thought he found a way,
to eliminate in one fell swoop
all the Christians of the nascent Church:
he massacred, tortured, and burned them.
But as Tertullian aptly observed,
"The blood of the martyrs is the seed of the Church."

To realize his purpose,
Jesus does not employ his enemies' tactics,
but asks Herod gently:
"Why do you want to kill me?";
the soldier who slaps him, "Why do you hit me?";
Saul of Tarsus, "Why do you persecute me?"

New Year Pastoral Letter (1995)

Some evenings,
when God looks at the world,
he has reason to despair.
In the face of this, however,
there remains the hope
of God: the Virgin Mary,
hope for the hopeless.
(B. Bro)[1]

We are counting on her maternal intercession
so that God makes 1995
a year of grace.

May God give each of us the opportunity
to be better in the coming year.
So that we can say,
in the depths of our souls, this wise prayer:

> "God, grant me
> the serenity to accept
> the things that I cannot change;
> the courage to change
> the things I can,

---

1. Editor's note: This quote comes from Bernard Bro, O.P., *Marie: Espoir de Dieu* (Paris: du Cerf, 1987).

and the wisdom to know
the difference
during the year of grace 1995."

It appears the coming year will be
a year of elections for the people of Zaire.
To speak of elections is to speak about discerning who is best equipped to lead.
For Christians, this choice must be rooted
in values that reflect the heart of Christ.
The choice will be Christian if it is rooted
first and foremost in justice and
universal charity:
this solidarity goes beyond tribal self-interest,
or money promised or given.
Because for a human being, there are certain values
we cannot compromise on.

A Greek poet magnificently expressed
the courage of such choice:

> "When Antigone learned of her brother's violent death
> and the tyrant Creon's prohibition
> on his burial,
> the girl consulted her heart.
> Although she knew that death awaited her,
> after bidding farewell to the light
> she would no longer see
> and the joys of motherhood she
> would never know,
> Antigone disobeyed the positive law
> of Creon, because she had
> within her heart a supreme,
> unwritten law, a divine law
> which demanded that she confer
> the last honors upon her brother.
> Her death was the price
> of her brotherly love."

As for us, it is the Spirit of Christ
which guides us. He is our reference.
Let us listen to him deeply
because he is at the heart of our hearts.

We have more than an unwritten law in our hearts;
God himself is within us,
and among us (Emmanuel).

Thus in 305, Saint Felicity, martyr of Carthage,
replied to the soldier who said:
"You groan from the pangs of childbirth,
how will you feel when you are in the arena,
thrown before furious bulls?"
She responded:
"I will not be alone, because the one for whom
I die will be with me in the struggle."

The spirit of Christ always reminds us
that neither blood, nor tribe,
nor material advantages
can be placed above
love of God and neighbor.

In the coming year,
may we, in solidarity with Christ,
wage the struggle not only for survival
but also growth in him.

> I therefore wish you
> a happy year,
> full of health
> in mind and body,
> peace in solidarity,
> and an unfailing holiness.
>
> May the Virgin Mary,
> who listened all her life

NEW YEAR PASTORAL LETTER

to the word of her Son,
lead us by the hand
throughout the New Year!

No matter what we face,
may the silent Word
be with us in our actions,
our sorrows, and our joys.
May we have a year of grace in 1995.

On Silence (May 1995)[1]

1. THE SOCIOLOGICAL MEANING OF SILENCE

SILENCE, WHILE IT MAY be the opposite of speech, is not devoid of meaning. We manifest a variety of feelings by being silent.

There is the silence of indifference, the haughty, contemptuous, reproachful, threatening silence. Many other internal dispositions come to mind. Let's concentrate on some of the more positive ones.

Silence is the language of respect. When we come across a funeral or a group sick people, we keep silent when we pass by them. There is no need to exchange words; silence is enough to express deference.

Silence is the language of awe before a magnificent spectacle: we cannot find the words. In the presence of an action of high moral value, we stay silent. Words cannot do what silence does. Admiration is expressed in silence.

When it comes to God, respect or admiration is called "adoration."

Silence is the language of attention: whoever wants to listen to a nearby conversation keeps silent. To keep silent in the presence of someone with whom you would like to speak shows your interest in his or her words. Silence in prayer is a sign of our attention to God.

Silence is the language of intimacy. "Happy are the friends who can be silent together," wrote Charles Péguy. To be silent together is indeed the privilege of those who, accustomed to keeping long silences, have become transparent to each other. They do not need words to understand each other. Words may even sometimes hinder their bond. It has reached a depth no human word can reach.

---

1. Editor's note: This excerpt is taken from Munzihirwa's 1995 archdiocesan pamphlet, "Sing to the Lord a New Song."

Two individuals who have shared everything in friendship can stand side by side without saying a word to each other. Their lives communicate even when words are in short supply. Nothing is more moving, for example, than the silence of the three companions, Eliphaz the Temanite, Bildad the Shuhite, and Zophar the Naamathite, who come to console Job. They sit next to him and stay for seven days and seven nights. At the sight of such great suffering, no one spoke to him (Job 2:12–13).

2. SILENCE AND LISTENING

It seems that in the Hungarian language, one and the same word, *hallgatni*, means both to listen and to be silent. In Italian, it's *sentire*, to identify with the speaker, to share what he says and does.

3. SILENCE AND RECEPTIVITY IN PRAYER

If in the beginning was the Word, and if all redemption is realized through his coming among us, it is clear that from the beginning of our salvation, there must be silence, the silence of listening, of welcome, of admiration.

Certainly, our words of gratitude, adoration, and supplication should correspond to the manifestation of the Word, but at the beginning, there is silence.

We could even say that the ability to live with a little silence characterizes the true believer and separates him from the world of unbelief.

There are many today who do not like silence. Faith gives the "new" man a love of silence, an ability to see beyond the spectacle, through a heart of charity, a heart capable of loving what may not be visible.

Like the Lord Jesus who, at dawn, climbed the mountain alone (Mark 1:35; Luke 4:42; 6:12; 12:9), we come to listen to the voice of the eternal Father.

4. VITAL EXPERIENCE

When Jesus returns from prayer joyful and relaxed, the disciples ask him: "Lord, teach us to pray" (Luke 11:1). We should remember the episode of Bethany as well (Luke 10:41–42).[2]

---

2. Editor's note: Munzihirwa refers here to the story of Mary and Martha: "But the

Moses spoke with God face to face: it is good to experience God's intimacy in prayer, to feel the Lord's breath.

To pray is not to isolate ourselves but to take responsibility for the world. The question that should spring from our praise is: "What does God want from us?"

Dialogue with God increases our readiness to lay aside our own interests and follow God's path, which consists of helping our brothers and sisters. "Not my will, but yours" (Luke 22:42).

Lord answered her, 'Martha, Martha, you are worried and distracted by many things; there is need of only one thing. Mary had chosen the better part [sitting at the Lord's feet listening to what he said], which will not be taken away from her.'"

PART III

The Rwandan Refugee Crisis

Homily from the Mass for Refugees and the Peace of All (July 24, 1994)

THE CRISIS IN RWANDA reveals our own crisis:

1. When the mass of refugees arrived, the authorities in Bukavu were completely absent. They only started to show up late, when the conscience of Christians had already been outraged by the behavior of those seeking to take advantage of the vulnerable position of the refugees and the confusion in the city. We must organize ourselves in order to defend our brothers.

We certainly understand the situation the civil authorities are facing. Their capacity has been greatly reduced, with no logistical support to draw upon. This is what happens when the country has been pillaged for thirty years!

2. We express our gratitude to the citizens who, despite their own poverty, are welcoming refugees into their homes. We especially thank the young people who have watched over the refugee city of Kadutu at night and protected them from criminals operating there.

3. After we heard about the behavior of the Civil Guard and other unscrupulous soldiers on the bridges of the Ruzizi, we sent two priests to find out what was happening at customs and immigration. According to their reports, while there were no major issues with the way agents treated pedestrians, the Civil Guard searched cars and seized goods, targeting not only citizens engaged in suspicious behavior, but also others who were clearly innocent.

4. At Ruzizi II,[1] a Protestant pastor witnessed horrible scenes. And in the city itself, a market of stolen goods from Rwanda has sprung up, offending the conscience of Christians. Thieves from Rwanda, wearing Zairian

---

1. Editor's note: Ruzizi II is one of the bridges where Zairian customs is located.

military uniforms, have stolen cars from their fellow refugees in Bagira, including the cars of priests.

Where are the representatives of justice? Where is law enforcement to ensure the protection of the people, especially the refugees and their belongings?

It is an understatement to say that some soldiers and officials are accomplices in such theft. It is worth remembering that neither thieves nor those who benefit from them will enter the kingdom of God if they do not repent and make restitution for their dishonest gains.[2] And we must include in this group all those who take advantage of this crisis to evict tenants so they can charge new tenants higher rents. We're also told that some corrupt soldiers lend (or "rent") their uniforms to criminals from Rwanda so that they can loot what little remains on the other side of the border.

We welcome all refugees without discrimination. But this also means that those we welcome must respect the good order, peace, and justice of those living here. Refugees must not be a part of the disorder, violence, and discrimination that are at the root of today's catastrophe.

5. The Christian conscience is thus outraged and condemns those who seek to enrich themselves by profiting from the misery and misfortune of others. We affirm the demand of Christians who call for the sacraments to be withheld from those engaged in such dishonest actions. Anyone who has stolen or bought goods at swindling prices must make amends if he wants to be in good standing with Jesus again.

6. We Christians cannot forget that Jesus, shortly after he was born, lived as a refugee in Egypt, and that the history of his ancestors included several exiles; we must not forget that Israel came out of slavery in Egypt.

As true Rwandan and Zairian Christians, let us therefore bear these events together, as they test our charity and spur our spiritual growth. Those seeking to exploit this situation will come out the worse, but true Christians will emerge from it renewed. For "there are things which can only be seen with eyes that have cried."

May the Lord wipe away our tears with the gift of peace!

---

2. Editor's note: Munzihirwa here alludes to 1 Cor 6:10: "thieves, the greedy, drunkards, revilers, robbers—none of these will inherit the kingdom of God."

May the Peace of Christ Dwell among Us (July 31, 1994)

WE KNOW THAT WITHIN every country, justice guarantees peace and security. But in our city of Bukavu, opportunistic citizens, including, unfortunately, those involved with so-called law enforcement and peacekeeping, have committed many injustices.

1. I hear that officers are seizing vehicles from the Rwandan refugees and selling them with impunity. Our basic human conscience, and our Christian conscience especially, condemn such acts. Neither the thief, nor those who purchase their ill-gotten goods, will enter the Kingdom of God if they do not return what they stole. The military prosecutor's office cannot become a market of stolen goods. And what about those who buy a cow, the poor's only source of wealth, at low prices or with old, worthless banknotes?

Let us listen to what the prophet Amos had to say about the greed of the merchants:

> Hear this, you that trample on the needy, and bring to ruin the poor of the land, saying, "When will the new moon be over so that we may sell grain, and the sabbath, so that that we may offer wheat for sale? We will make the ephah small and the shekel great, and practice deceit with false balances, buying the poor for silver and the needy for a pair of sandals, and selling the sweepings of the wheat." The Lord has sworn by the pride of Jacob: "Surely I will never forget any of their deeds. Shall not the land tremble on this account and everyone mourn who lives in it?" (Amos 8:4–8)

2. I also hear that they are going to forcibly repatriate the refugees, or at least force UNHCR not to assist them in order to compel them to return. Such an act would be a crime against humanity if we do not help to establish the real peace and security for the refugees who agree to return home.

3. The victor cannot be the sole arbiter and judge of the defeated in war. Victory does not necessarily mean justice. What should we make of a party that goes to war to combat the abuses of a single party only to set up five years of its own dictatorship? We know that in Africa, all dictatorships, from Sekou Touré to Habyarimana, have first given themselves five years before holding free elections!

What would have happened at the end of the Second World War if Russia, France, and England had been left alone to judge the Nazis? I think nearly all of the German leaders would have been executed. It took the Americans, less passionate in this matter perhaps, to oversee the famous Nuremberg tribunal. This weakened the immediate desire for revenge and opened the possibility for reconciliation between former enemies.

We ask the world powers to quickly facilitate talks between the Rwandans, just as we tell Rwandans themselves that it is more humane to forgive than seek revenge.

May the peace of Christ, who died forgiving, guide our minds and our hearts.

Letter to UN Secretary General Boutros Boutros-Ghali (August 2, 1994)

Mr. Secretary General,

Regarding: the failure to assist Rwandan refugees in mortal danger in Bukavu, Zaire

Since the massive influx of refugees in Bukavu on July 18, the response of the High Commissioner of Refugees (UNHCR) has proven ineffective due to a lack of organization and, perhaps, a failure of will on the part of some of its workers. Refugees are starting to die from hunger in the city, denied the assistance of even a little food on the pretext that they are not in a camp, even as they are hindered in their attempt to reach those camps!

On top of this, we are hearing through the media that international organizations and certain western powers want to forcibly repatriate the refugees, or at least pressure UNHCR not to assist them in order to force them to return to their country.

On behalf of the entire Catholic community of Bukavu and human rights organizations, we denounce this act as a crime against humanity if it does not help establish true peace in Rwanda and security for refugees who agree to return.

Given that Rwanda is being destroyed by extremists on both sides, we ask today's great powers to facilitate talks between all Rwandans so they can find a balanced solution.

Please accept, Mr. Secretary General, my very highest regards.

Do the Nations Want to Serve the Great Lakes Region of Africa? The Church Faces the Challenge of Violence and Hypocrisy (August 3, 1994)

THE VIOLATION OF HUMAN rights has made our continent a continent of refugees. Of the fifteen million refugees worldwide, more than six million are in Africa.

Particularly atrocious wars are unfolding in the Sudan. Few speak out against the tragedies, and no action is being taken to prevent the genocide of Christian and animist tribes in the South, where the Islamist regime of the North seeks to impose its totalitarian hegemony. Since 1960, refugees have been in Zaire, Uganda, and Ethiopia. There is also talk of Libya and Saudi Arabia planning to spread their influence throughout East and Central Africa, financing the arms trade with the aim of destabilizing these countries.

Angola has been entrenched in an ideologically driven ethnic war for almost twenty years: so many dead, so many crippled, so much impoverishment, all because of the ambition of Jonas Savimbi and his supporters, who appear to want to empty the country so they can have unlimited access to the riches of the land and sea! Refugees from this country have been in Zaire and Zambia since the beginning of this endless war.

Liberia, once so prosperous, has been in agony for six years. It is not even discussed anymore. War has become endemic. Who started it? Who profits from it?

Since 1975, Mozambique has suffered the same fate as Angola: a struggle for power and arms trafficking that has had no other effect than the gradual extermination of an entire population. Refugees have scattered to such places as South Africa and Malawi.

DO THE NATIONS WANT TO SERVE THE GREAT LAKES REGION

In Zaire, political turmoil and the collapse of the economy have been accompanied by a criminal racism against Kasaians, starting in Shaba. Who took interest in this proliferation of misery and displacement? The country did nothing! The nations do not care!

We are particularly troubled by what is happening in the hills near our home of Zaire. In Burundi and Rwanda, fratricidal wars are still raging; their consequences are incalculable. We thought it would just be a gust of wind, but in Rwanda, the violence became a persistent storm that the nation's best and brightest have been unable to stop. The international community acts as if it merely "watched" the forces of death unleash themselves, but it is hard not to wonder if there was some hidden, well-coordinated plan hatched in some dark place.

In Burundi, despite multiple investigations since October 1993, we still do not know who orchestrated the assassination of President Ndadaye; there were soldiers who carried out the plan, but who came up with it? Who gave the orders, who funded the action, who frustrated the investigations, and for what reasons? At the same time, there was a related plan that provoked the ensuing massacres: Who prepared the plan? Why was it executed with such cruelty on such a vast scale? For what reasons? What hypocrisy! Everywhere the dead are mourned; more than 25 percent of the population is "displaced," living in fear and misery; neither the violence nor the conspiring has reached an end.

In Rwanda, a foreign-supported war without a clear rationale began four years ago; but then another plan was hatched: the assassination of President Habyarimana, the details of which remain unknown, followed by countless killings carried out by soldiers and paramilitary groups, complete with lists of intended victims and terrible vendettas, culminating in conflict between the most violent elements and enormous physical destruction. To what end? Hypocrisy reigns supreme! Everywhere the dead are mourned; the majority of the population is "displaced"; a small minority tries to reconstruct a political system in part of the country. Thirty years of work is destroyed for what? Distant countries think they are defending the rights of the majority; other countries want to defend the rights of the minority; each claims to build a just democracy, but neither side wants democracy. A Western-style democracy is not easily achieved in the socio-cultural context of central Africa; instead, we see the grasping for absolute power to acquire or secure "privileges," no matter the cost to the people, no matter the risk of provoking conflict in the future. Why?

Christians: Even if we cannot prevent violence, we must always disapprove of it; we must know how to say NO, an absolute no to it. Even if we fail to unravel the Gordian knot of hypocrisy, we must always denounce it: we must know how to say NO, an equally absolute no to it as well. Then we must try to overcome the violence and hypocrisy, awakening a better vision of this profoundly troubled world, where the wheat and chaff always grow together. Good grain exists, in large numbers and of astonishing quality. For proof, we need only look to the recent statements of many Tutsis who came looking for refuge in the Kivus, saying they owed their lives to some courageous Hutus who acted with a basic respect for life, for man, and for the brotherhood of all human beings in Christ (see the testimonials that Philippe de Dorlodot gathered for his July 1994 report in Bukavu;[1] or the "signs of hope" that have been reported in both Rwanda and Burundi over the past six months. One could cite similar examples of Tutsis protecting Hutus, such as the Tutsi mother who protected twenty students fleeing a massacre at their school). The good grain is Christ living today in the midst of the chaff, in the darkest hours of human tragedy. It is an attitude that steps back in tolerance, sensitive to the power of love to open the way to disarmament, providing a surer foundation upon which to rebuild. A wise man once said, "There are things which can only be seen with eyes that have cried"; at a certain remove from the normal human passions, we find hope in him who is the Way, the Truth, and the Life.

In these days when we continue to dig mass graves, where misery and disease spread across thousands of kilometers of roads, tracks, trails, hills, refuges, and camps, we are particularly challenged by the cry of Christ on the cross: "Father, forgive them for they know not what they do!" At certain moments, the mercy of God, which cuts the cords of revenge, seems to disturb militants of all kinds; after all, it is mercy that ultimately ends all vendettas. The Lord our God forgave; he asks us to forgive. Such forgiveness is the logic of salvation. Augustine of Hippo was able to say his brothers, "You say you are sons of God. If you refuse to forgive, why do you still desire his inheritance? It can only be given through the only begotten Son, who died forgiving." Christians, we must, like John the Baptist, be heralds of the "Good News of Forgiveness," repeating, in our words and deeds, "Behold the Lamb of God, who takes away the sin of the world."

---

1. Editor's note: Philippe de Dorlodot, a Catholic priest, was actively involved in Bukavu at the time. He later edited a large collection of civil society responses to the Rwandan refugee crisis entitled *Réfugiés rwandais à Bukavu au Zaïre: De nouveau Palestiniens?*

Strengthened by this faith in Jesus Christ, the Church must be a servant of justice and peace; this service constitutes the mission of the Church, especially in Africa today.

Rebuilding a country like Rwanda will require a sustainable peace of mind and body; here, as with any other place, we must dare to do it. It will be the fruit of dialogue and lasting reconciliation; it will demand a long process of negotiation led by individuals who are aware of the common interests of all the citizens of their nation. A nation is above all a daily expression of "the will to live together," forgetting the shadows of the past, doing everything possible to avoid a dictatorship of either the majority or minority. When it is not defensive, war is always misguided, an individual or group's attempt to seize or maintain power through violence. "You think you are fighting for your country, when in fact you're fighting to defend the interests of the bourgeoisie," observed one European citizen who analyzed life after the great wars of the twentieth century.

Those who have been displaced are victims of violence and the cunning, cynical intoxication that drives people to an intolerance of difference. It was the same with the tower of Babel! Weapons must be silenced, so the wandering masses can have time to collect themselves and reflect upon the causes of the storm, so that people of integrity can draw upon their deepest convictions to serve the common good and lay the seeds for a "new democracy," culturally rooted in our African realities. May the arms trade cease, may the demagoguery within our countries and the jockeying for international influence come to an end. Let governments emerge that reflect the free and conscious will of people who want to live in peace again.

History provides us with many lessons of this. At certain moments, forgiveness and reconciliation appear impossible, but we always come to realize that life will remain unbearable without them. Lest they give up on the future, all nations feel the need for amnesty at some point. Without reconciliation, there would be no Asia or Europe; the victors and vanquished of WWII came together to celebrate the newfound peace. It was due to individuals who, during the conflagration of war, had the foresight to draw up a plan of understanding and collaboration for the establishment of a more solid peace, rooted in shared economic interests and grassroots cultural exchange. Thus they prevented those at the top from continuing to sacrifice the people in their thirst for power.

Looking at events with a more analytical and objective eye, we see that while there may be violence and revenge on both sides of the conflict, innocent and peaceful people only suffer as a result. It is without their knowledge and against their will that those seeking power have devised nefarious schemes to achieve their ends: they seek power for themselves at the expense of the people.

We also see that in many ethnic conflicts, there are people on both sides who deplore this madness, and do what they can to save lives, even if they are labeled traitors, sometimes suffering the fate of those they helped or tried to save. When we look at history, we discover that many of the Germans who opposed the Nazi regime suffered the same fate as the Jews they tried to save.

In Germany, it was necessary to distinguish a German from a Nazi; in Lebanon, a Muslim from an Islamist; in Rwanda, a Hutu should be distinguished from members of the *Interahamwe* or the presidential guard who sought to maintain power through genocide; so too a Tutsi should be distinguished from certain members of the RPF who want to take power by force and eliminate all opposition. Both sides kill "for power."

The massacres perpetrated by the presidential guard in order to avenge the president provoked indignation in every Christian of conscience. But revenge is not to be taken lightly. The premeditated assassination of three bishops and priests is just a sign of many more planned "eliminations." This is why our conscience must firmly oppose all vendettas: young people are killed under the pretext that they were militia members, thereby establishing the peace of the cemetery. What can we expect from a government that shamelessly favors a return to illiteracy, as was heard on RPF radio. People from the northern areas, particularly Ruhengeri, have witnessed revenge killings by RPF soldiers who claim to be a liberation army. Some peasants who fled to Bugesera, near the destroyed bridge over the Nyabarango, were executed with machine guns. At this rate, Rwanda will be deserted, even though thousands of former refugees are converging around Kigali and RPF–controlled areas. The hundreds of thousands of Rwandans in refugee camps in Tanzania, Burundi, and South and North Kivu are raising a clamor that no one will be able to ignore.

The UN peacekeeping force in Kigali has failed to remain neutral in carrying out its mission. The French Operation Turquoise declared its partisan plans from the beginning; it saved some lives but, blinded by its ideology of Western-style democracy, did not take into account all aspects of the situation; it could not handle the movement of hundreds of thousands of people reduced to misery. It no longer knows how to take a step forward or backward without sacrificing further lives. The nations pity the countless victims scattered throughout the Great Lakes countries; there is a lot of good will, and the provision of humanitarian aid attests to the human genius for generosity when it comes to emergency relief. But who will intervene "for tomorrow"? Who will expose the plans of the protected few who continue to turn the "gristmill of the poor"? Some say that an international intervention "force" is necessary to protect the "rights of all," because the dice are loaded both in Burundi and Rwanda, even if the situations are distinct. Where are the levers of dialogue and truth?

Disciples of Christ can only claim to be followers of Christ if they have the honesty and courage to be "servants of all," and stand in solidarity with the poor. We are told that love is proven through action. If there are refugees at our doorstep, let us create an atmosphere of compassion where the flowers of mutual assistance can bloom. We must know how to welcome every brother and sister, without distinction of race or social class, without making accusations or showing contempt. If the possibility of refugees returning home emerges, we must be servants of mutual love, dialogue, mercy, and reconciliation at all levels. If a new future of national coexistence is to be born, Christ's disciples must be leaven in the dough; not militants of intolerant parties, but bearers of the Spirit. It is the community of Pentecost, one that, with Mary, increasingly welcomes the forces of love and life in the Spirit of Jesus, that will be the seed of great new things in the Great Lakes region at the dawning of the year 2000.

Letter of Protest (August 23, 1994)

To the Regional Governor
To the UNHCR representative in Bukavu
To the representative of Caritas International

Subject: Expression of growing concern over the gaps in assistance provided to the Rwandan disaster victims and the effects of this upon the Zairian population in the city of Bukavu and surrounding area.

1. We flew over the refugee camps, which already contain over three hundred thousand people. We met a caravan heading to the Mulungu site.[1] Jesuit Father Minani and a few companions were the only ones guiding them from the College Alfajiri,[2] where some twenty-five thousand refugees were living under the stars, in the rain, for over a month. When one thousand evacuate, two thousand more arrive . . . and so it goes to until today. They are materially destitute, but above all they suffer spiritually because they were forced to leave everything by a group of men who wanted to seize power by force.

The statements made on Rwandan radio do not seem to correspond to reality on the ground. Among the refugees who have arrived here, there are some who have recently fled areas controlled by the RPF. They saw them rounding up people and forcing them to denounce the guilty; young people are selected and led to their death. How do you expect them to return to their homeland under such circumstances? When there is no amnesty? When there is no meeting between the two parties? This would simply be

---

1. Editor's note: Mulungu, roughly twenty miles from Bukavu, was the site of one of the largest refugee camps during this period.

2. Editor's note: College Alfajiri is the headquarters of the Jesuits in Bukavu and the site of a prestigious secondary school.

surrendering to the arbitrariness of the victor. "Woe to the vanquished," goes the saying from Rome of the Caesars.

2. Bukavu and the surrounding Bushi areas are overpopulated with one million inhabitants, or 250 people per square kilometer. For many years there have been attempts to alleviate the situation. Now there are nearly two million Rwandans in need of food and shelter. Soon they will be looking for a place to stay. They are already occupying the schools, with the start of classes just a month away. Of course the population welcomes these refugees in distress. But will they be willing to give up their future?

3. We call upon the humanitarian organizations assisting the refugees to do everything in their power, even through extraordinary means, to provide relief from this disaster which afflicts both the impoverished and homeless Rwandan refugees and the local Zairian population. Both have lost their sense of ordinary life, their natural environment, and are now threatened by epidemics that spread through the unsanitary conditions that are increasingly common everywhere.

And where is the Zairian government? Where is the regional governor? They don't organize anything and leave the population without a political or military authority! What is the international community doing to bring real and much-needed peace to Rwanda after its atrocious civil war?

We are counting on everyone. Let us all obey the law of love unceasingly preached by Christ, which is the path to true and lasting peace.

S.O.S. from the Archbishop of Bukavu on Behalf of the Refugees (September 8, 1994)

THE RAINY SEASON HAS arrived! And most refugees have no sheeting, tents, or blankets.

1. Their distress is great, but conditions in Rwanda are not conducive to their return. Indeed, there are clandestine or summary executions of Hutus who try to go back. An arbitrary military reigns supreme. The authorities in Kigali do not deny this; they say that it is due to the collapse of administrative and legal structures and the lack of social support. This allows the military, the only masters in the land, to take revenge with impunity.

2. It is imperative that goods that have come into Zaire from Rwanda be restored to their rightful owners. This is only fair: Zaire cannot become a den of thieves. We are ashamed and saddened by the actions of many soldiers in Bukavu. Every thief must make restitution.

3. But to whom should these goods be returned? By what standard of justice and equity? These goods and the money that would have been deposited in Zaire are the product of the labor of people who have lost everything. Since they no longer possess the goods they produced, they are entitled to protection, especially from the great powers who could have prevented this tragedy but allowed it to happen.

A small group of people associated with the late President Habyarimana seized control of the economy and abandoned these impoverished people, who today find themselves in even greater distress.

Do the authorities in Kigali who have claimed these assets really have the right to do so before God, when the masses of people who produced them are languishing in misery here? The people and their goods must return together. Otherwise, it would be like an armed robber broke into your home, kicked you out of your house, and then demanded you bring him any remaining items you may have kept.

It is disconcerting to see the United Nations allow adventurers to take up arms, occupy the country, and, once in power, subjugate the population. It's a reign of arbitrary terror. It is the return of colonial power, when there were states without nations.

Augustine tells a story that speaks to the situation in Rwanda today: "One day, a famous pirate who had ransomed people on the Mediterranean Sea was captured. He was brought before Alexander the Great, who asked him, 'What makes you think you can attack people on the sea, killing or capturing them to take their property?' He coolly responded, 'What's the difference between you and me? I'm called a pirate because I have a small boat, but because you have an entire fleet, you are called emperor!'"[1]

This suggests that states like Zaire and Rwanda have become little more than robbers on a large scale.

Still, we call for our Nation's recovery, as South Africa and other countries have recently done.

---

1. Editor's note: Augustine tells this story in *City of God* book IV.4.

Insecurity in Bukavu (September 8, 1994)

I.
For the past month, the population of Bukavu, that stricken city that some want to bury, has been living in fear of Zairian soldiers consumed by the desire to steal the refugees' possessions. They use this situation as an opportunity to steal from Zairians as well.

The number of those donning uniforms and feigning to be soldiers is multiplying, and they are colluding with members of the army. There is no shortage of examples. A few days ago, soldiers in Civil Guard uniforms set out to raid Dr. Mitéo. He was able to call for help. The city commander came to the scene. He caught them in the act, and called the commander of the Civil Guard so that he could see the disorder in his unit. These men, who carry guns in their hands, terrorize us with their lack of discipline. Don't they know that they are our children, our brothers who should love us?

On the other hand, history teaches us that soldiers who seek to pillage are not fit to defend their homeland. The enemy will catch them stealing instead of being on the watch. That is why self-respecting armies do not tolerate theft or mutiny.

Pillage becomes a temptation for soldiers when they are left to their own devices. A prince in the Middle Ages said that there is a demon in the heart of every soldier, but this demon is multiplied fourfold whenever there is opportunity to pillage! In order to discourage his soldiers from pillaging, Alexander the Great, King of Macedonia and greatest military strategist of Greek antiquity, once let his soldiers follow their instincts, then asked them to gather their loot, which he inspected and then set on fire, telling them, "We have other cities to conquer; you will be able to celebrate when the whole world is under our dominion. Forward, march!" He ended up conquering the East, from Greece to India, achieving the greatest empire of the time. After his untimely death, his generals divided the empire among themselves.

Discipline is the foundation of all military success. Our soldiers, who once conquered Tabora, Mahenge, and Saio, fled—despite having modern equipment—before a small group of rebels at Kolwezi in 1978. They did the same during the 1964 rebellion by a force that had no other means of defense than the belief that a magic potion and the chant *"Mulele mayi!"* made them invincible. Fortunately, Bukavu has retained the names of those who believed in military valor: Mulamba Place and Vangu Place.[1]

Yesterday, a Rundi commando came to taunt Zaire by strolling defiantly through the refugee camps. Where were the Zairian soldiers? Probably at the market! Isn't it time that our soldiers realized the value of a national army? That they were born civilians and most of them will die civilians? And if they die as soldiers, will they die in service of their country or as common thieves? The nation remembers the names of Major Vangu, Colonel Tshatshi, d'Ebeya.... May the future honor others!

II.
Soldiers are Christians too. The Gospel tells us that when soldiers asked John the Baptist, "What must we do to save our souls?" he replied to them, "Respect justice and be content with your wages." The Gospel also commends the example of a centurion who was the leader of troops. Jesus said that he hadn't found such faith in all of Israel. Throughout history, there has been no shortage of soldiers who preferred to suffer punishment rather than carry out an unjust order.

The Second Vatican Council praises soldiers who die in defense of their brothers and who protect their lives with integrity and love. The people of Kinshasa shower the traffic officers who are kind and effective with gifts. They don't need to ask for the famous *madeso sa bana*.[2]

---

1. Editor's note: Munzihirwa refers here and in the following paragraph to decorated military leaders who served in the National Congolese Army during the 1960s.
2. Editor's note: Literally, "beans for the children," a way of asking for a bribe.

Those who are tempted by corruption only have to remember this story from the eighteenth century: "Three conscripts who didn't care for God put on their uniforms to go to war. Along the way, they saw an imposing statue of the Virgin Mary in a village. They said to themselves, 'Let's practice shooting at it.' So they did. The first hit the shoulder, the second the throat, and the third the chest. Satisfied, they went away singing. The time for battle arrived. The one who shot the statue in the throat was shot in the throat; the one who shot her in the chest was shot in the chest. Both died. A mortar fragment shattered the third one's shoulder. And it was he who, on his hospital bed, told the story of their unfortunate adventure."

We may not see it every day, but justice does eventually come around.

Letter to Misereor Representative (September 19, 1994)

To Mr. Karl Wirtz
Representative of Misereor[1]

Concerning: Rwandan refugees in Bukavu: implications for the region and conditions for their rapid return home

I would like to thank you for your cooperation and the emergency relief you are providing to alleviate the misery of our Rwandan brothers and sisters.

But in the face of the crisis that we are currently experiencing in the Kivus, there are two things that organizations coming to our aid need to bear in mind.

1. Our region is devastated

The Bushi region surrounding Bukavu, where a million Rwandans have gathered, already had a population of one and a half million before their arrival.

At 250 people per square kilometer, it is the highest population density in Africa, a density even greater than that of Rwanda. The arrival of this great mass of refugees will therefore lead, in the short or medium term, to a new humanitarian crisis.

The people of Bushi have already exhausted their provisions by sharing them with the refugees, and the next harvest will not be until February 1995. To bridge the gap, food assistance will be indispensable for the immediate future.

---

1. Editor's note: Misereor is the German Catholic Bishops' Organization for Development Cooperation.

Fields ordinarily used for cultivation are currently occupied by the refugees: it would only be just to provide some modest compensation to the affected population for what they have endured.

Several schools have been damaged; repairs and new equipment are needed so they can function as they did before.

Trees need to be replanted everywhere, and the crisis is only just beginning. The rain has started again and the trees will not take root for many years. Meanwhile, the refugees need firewood. What should be done?

2. The key issue is the rapid return of the refugees to Rwanda, their homeland.

They are waiting for this, but on terms consistent with dignity and justice. They refuse the serfdom that prevailed in Rwanda only a few decades ago. They want to return to the land they farmed before others arrived in the region.

They want to return but are afraid of an arbitrary military. The military, being the only authority in power, claims the right to kill, and does in fact kill. Apart from their presence, there is no civil or judicial institution that could defend the population.

At a meeting in Butare on September 5, the Rwandan bishops asked a representative of the RPF about this and he confirmed this state of affairs. The RPF deplores this situation.

One fears that the situation of the Hutu population in Rwanda will become like that of the Palestinians, who have endured the law of the strong for many years.

Meanwhile, it seems certain European circles have been manipulated into condemning the Hutus *en bloc*. We see the media portray the RPF in almost angelic terms! It is time that the true champions of democracy express their point of view on the situation, a lawless one that currently prevails in Rwanda and makes the refugees tremble.

Have the international commissions conducted investigations in the region of Ruhengeri and Byumba where the war started in 1990? Do the champions of democracy know that there are two lists of criminals circulating in Kigali, one official and another unofficial?

In the face of this situation, we feel it is essential that humanitarian organizations use their influence to demand from the new government in Kigali a negotiated political solution guaranteeing peace and justice for all.

LETTER TO MISEREOR REPRESENTATIVE

In order to avoid a new humanitarian crisis in Bushi—and the risk of generating unprecedented conflicts—facilitating the just return of refugees to their country is a matter of the greatest urgency. It seems to us that the essential condition for this is the creation of the actual rule of law in Rwanda.

Homily from Mass at Saio Military Camp (October 15, 1994)

TODAY'S GOSPEL SPEAKS ABOUT the greatness of service, even the humblest kind. It is God whom we serve in our brothers.

Today, we reflect together on the nobility of military service, properly understood and performed, as a service to the country and nation.

Why are Zairians in general afraid of the military, when the soldier is their brother? Why do they fear him rather than love him? It is because bad soldiers are tarnishing the image of the army.

There are good soldiers, and history gives us the names of illustrious soldiers. The gospel also gives us the example of saints, and the whole history of the Church is filled with heroes who risked their lives to save their country or died to spare the living from slaughter. This is what it means to die for one's country.

1. LET'S FIRST SEE WHAT THE GOSPEL SAYS

In chapter 8, verse 5, Saint Matthew recounts the healing of a centurion's servant (centurions typically commanded one hundred soldiers, the smallest unit of the Roman army). This centurion said to the Lord, "Lord, I am not worthy to have you come under my roof; but only speak the word, and my servant will be healed. For I also am a man under authority, with soldiers under me; and I say to one, 'Go,' and he goes, and to another, 'Come,' and he comes, and to my slave, 'Do this,' and the slave does it." And the Gospel tells us that in hearing this, Jesus was amazed and said to his followers, "Truly I tell you, in no one in Israel have I found such faith."

In chapter 3, verse 14, Saint Luke tells us what John the Baptist preached to the soldiers who asked, "What must we do to be saved?" And

John the Baptist said to them, "Do no violence or harm to anyone and be content with your wages."[1]

In chapter 10 of the Acts of the Apostles, Saint Luke tells the wonderful story of the first pagan who became a Christian: "In Caesarea there was a man named Cornelius, a centurion of the Italian Cohort, as it was called. He was a devout man who feared God with all his household; he gave alms generously to the people and prayed constantly to God." God sends Peter to this man. And Cornelius and his entire family were the first pagans to be baptized.

2. WHAT DOES THE CHURCH THINK OF THE ARMY?

In its Social Constitution, "The Church in the Modern World," the Second Vatican Council speaks of safeguarding peace in the world.

> [The] achievement of peace requires a constant mastering of passions and the vigilance of the legitimate authority. But this is not enough. This peace on earth cannot be obtained unless personal well-being is safeguarded and men freely and trustingly share with one another the riches of their inner spirits and talents. A firm determination to respect other men and peoples and their dignity, as well as the studied practice of brotherhood are absolutely necessary for the establishment of peace.[2]

Vatican II also asked all nations to put a stop to the inhumanity of wars. But we have to recognize that, in the present state of the world, war has not disappeared from human affairs. The Council adds that

> as long as the danger of war remains and there is no competent and sufficiently powerful authority at the international level, governments cannot be denied the right to legitimate defense once every means of peaceful settlement has been exhausted. State authorities and other who share public responsibility have a duty to conduct such grave matters soberly and to protect the welfare of the people entrusted to their care. But it is one thing to undertake military action for the just defense of the people, and something else to seek the subjugation of other nations.

---

1. Editor's translation of Munzihirwa's original.

2. Editor's note: Quotations in this and the following paragraphs come from *Gaudium et Spes*, para. 78–79.

The mere possession of arms does not legitimize any use of this force for political or military ends. "Nor by the same token, does the mere fact that war has unhappily begun mean that all is fair between the warring parties. Those too who devote themselves to the military service of their country should regard themselves as the agents of security and freedom of peoples. As long they fulfill this role properly, they are making a genuine contribution to the establishment of peace." We must underscore "properly" here and invite our military brothers and sons to examine their conscience: How are they treating us? How are they behaving?

Our public memory preserves the example of the soldier Vangu, who fought against the mercenaries of the UN; there is a memorial dedicated to him called "*l'Essence*." We also remember Colonel Mulamba, who, surrounded by key figures from this region, courageously helped to rout the rebels in 1965. On the other hand, we forget those who, in 1967, cowardly abandoned the region into the hands of [Jean] Schramme and who returned in November only to loot what remained.

Let the army currently stationed in Kivu ask itself: Could you achieve the victory at Saio? At Asosa? Gambela?[3] Could you save us?

Without discipline, a solder is not fit to defend his country, because a soldier who plunders his country no longer has any sense of his homeland. He lives in confusion. Wasn't it the case in 1978 that Zaire could only defend itself against a handful of poorly armed rebels with the help of the French and Moroccans?[4]

To defend the country, you first have to love it, from its youngest to oldest members, then be trained in the necessary discipline and skill to defend them. So love your Zairian parents and brothers who are counting on you to guarantee their freedom in peace. Respect also the strangers who are among us. This is what African hospitality and dignity requires.

Do not forget that not so long ago, some of those who are refugees today helped to stem the first advance of the Mulelists on the Bugarama bridge towards Bukavu. As Christians, what is happening in Rwanda and Burundi cannot leave us indifferent. There's a hymn that says, "When war comes and our neighbor dies, it's the passion of Christ rekindled each time."

---

3. Editor's note: Munzihirwa refers to three key battles in Ethiopia that the Allies won with the support of Congolese troops during WWII.

4. Editor's note: Munzihirwa refers here to the Shaba rebellion which took place in May 1978.

HOMILY FROM MASS AT SAIO MILITARY CAMP

We greatly appreciated the army's gesture on September 15, when it helped to clean the city so that our children could safely return to school with dignity.

Our hope is that every soldier inspires confidence and sympathy within us, instead of horror, indignation, and fear.

God loves good soldiers. The Church has canonized the likes of Saint Maurice, Saint George, Saint Martin . . . .

Letter to Cardinal Danneels (President, Pax Christi) and Monsignor Delaporte (Justice and Peace, France) (January 16, 1995)

Your Eminence and Excellency,

Concerning: Appeal for increased support for a negotiated solution in Rwanda that would allow the refugees to return home

Since July 1994, there have been more than two million Rwandan Hutu refugees in Zaire, four hundred thousand of whom are in the diocese of Bukavu. They live under increasingly distressed conditions: the distribution of food occurs sporadically and it is difficult to find wood for cooking. Several humanitarian organizations are leaving. Rwanda changed its currency at the beginning of January, and because it closed its borders, the refugees weren't able to take advantage of the currency exchange, losing what little money they had left.

The vast majority of refugees want to return to their country, but are unable to do so: the conditions for their return are not in place. They are afraid of being imprisoned based upon a simple accusation on unproven facts, or being killed if they try to reclaim their property. According to witnesses in Rwanda, the massacres continue there, and are even intensifying. It is estimated that between five to ten thousand people are assassinated in Rwanda every month. And in recent days, some refugees have continued to arrive here.

There is no other peaceful solution to this crisis than a meeting of all Rwandans aimed at negotiating a fair political solution. A lot of work and discussion created the hope that this meeting would happen last November. That hope was destroyed when the Rwandan government received financial aid from some Western governments. There is reason to question aid that is given to a minority that took power through arms. It helps Rwanda, but neglects the Rwandans who are languishing in the camps, in great distress and without a future. . . . The refugees are mainly a young population. Idle and without basic necessities, these young people will look for a violent solution here in Kivu and Rwanda. And the consequences for the local population are severe: the refugees occupy what was formerly farmland in an already overpopulated region.

To leave two million Rwandans languishing in Zaire is a crime against humanity. Moreover, it is unacceptable that Western democracies provide unconditional support to a regime in Kigali that prohibits free speech and prevents the return of nearly a third of its population. Therefore I call upon you to use all your moral authority as primate of Belgium and president of Pax Christi International, and as president of the French Justice and Peace Commission, respectively. Can the Church in Belgium and France not launch an urgent appeal to the West to put pressure on the Rwandan leaders, Hutu and Tutsi, to find a political solution that allows the refugees to return?

Please accept, your Eminence and Excellency, my kindest regards.

The Social Situation in Bukavu Today (April 28, 1995)

THERE IS A FOOD shortage. The mountainous region of the Kivus, with its 250 inhabitants per square kilometer, no longer has enough land to feed people sufficiently. It has almost been a year since we welcomed the Rwandan refugees. And there are still new refugees arriving every day from Rwanda.

UNHCR has done its best to feed them. But things have now stalled. At the border, Rwanda and Burundi prevent trucks from the UN's World Food Program from bringing food to the refugees. They don't have clothes to wear or food to eat. Now we fear a war of the hungry, especially given that there are many armed young people among them.

For the third time, the Rwandan army made incursions during the night on the lake near Bukavu, in the territorial waters of Zaire, near the governor's residence:

- The first time, three Zairian fishermen were killed.
- The second time another Zairian was killed.
- The third time a refugee camp in Birava, close to the lake, was attacked. There were thirty-four people killed on the spot, but counting those who later died from serious injuries in the hospitals, there were fifty Rwandans and ten Zairians dead.

It seems to me that this is both revenge and a provocation meant to deflect attention away from the massacres taking place in Rwanda. Recently in Kibeho, witnesses spoke of six to eight thousand dead.[1]

---

1. Editor's note: Munzihirwa refers here to the Kibeho massacre. See p. 20n78 in the introduction.

THE SOCIAL SITUATION IN BUKAVU TODAY

At the beginning, we were all shocked by the genocide of the Tutsi, but today the world seems to keep silent about the genocide of the Hutu. It seems generally agreed that an armed minority, in order to stay in power, can exterminate an unarmed majority. What logic!

However, those who supply the funds and weapons can stop these rising deaths. Why does the West never talk about Museveni, the president of Uganda, who continues to provide arms and soldiers to Tutsis in Rwanda and Burundi?

Mobutu seems to have gotten scared when we denounced his alliance with the fleeing Rwandan army. But if he sees others doing it safely on the other side, won't he be tempted to do it again?

The church is deeply alarmed by this collective evil. We preach forgiveness and call for dialogue, but from Rwanda, we hear only the sound of weapons and calls for revenge.

May the Virgin Mary, who sheds her maternal tears over Rwanda, rejoice one day that peace has returned to her children. On both sides, there are men and women who want to meet and dialogue. But the extremists are suffocating them.

Letter to the Christian Consortium for Central Africa (April 28, 1995)[1]

BRIEFING REGARDING SOME URGENT problems concerning the Rwandan refugees

1. You are no doubt aware of recent developments that have affected the Rwandan refugees in our region: in mid-March, the media announced that the budget for the refugees in Zaire would be cut off at the end of April, and, more recently, fifty-three trucks carrying food were blocked in Cyangugu and Kigali in order to starve the refugees. How can Caritas International work with the World Food Program to ensure that, on the one hand, the budget that was allocated for the Rwandan refugees for the entire year (and not just to the end of April) is disbursed, and on the other, that the food actually reaches them? You know that rations in the camps have been reduced by half, from eighteen hundred to nine hundred calories a day. Given that a great shortage afflicts the local population that has nothing left to share, what will happen in Bukavu when all of these refugees are starving?

2. You know about the suffering of prisoners in Rwanda. People locked in containers are "found" dead. Prisons are overcrowded: four to six people per square meter. Thousands of women and children are detained under these conditions on the basis of simple accusation or revenge. It is essentially a depopulation strategy. What can Justice and Peace and other groups do to put a stop to this intolerable situation?

---

1. Editor's note: The Christian Consortium for Central Africa, or CCAC, was a Brussels-based peacebuilding network that included Caritas International, the International Cooperation for Development and Solidarity, Justice and Peace Europe, and Pax Christi International. See de Dorlodot, *Réfugiés rwandais à Bukavu au Zaïre*, 196n59.

LETTER TO THE CHRISTIAN CONSORTIUM FOR CENTRAL AFRICA

What can Justice and Peace do to ensure that those who are truly guilty—we know most of them—are arrested and judged?

3. You know that on January 16, 1995, I wrote Cardinal Danneels, president of Pax Christi International, and Mgr. Delaporte of the Justice and Peace Commission France. Having received no response other than a brief acknowledgment of receipt, can you tell me what Pax Christi has undertaken: What pressure did it exert on western states to bring about peace negotiations in Rwanda? The status quo will only lead to a deadlier war in the long term. On April 11, there was an RPF raid on Birava in Zaire, and there were other attacks on the lake before that. Isn't this a premeditated provocation? What can Pax Christi and others do to stop the arms trade?

4. What do you intend to do in response to the monstrous killings at Kibeho, shown on TV, which reveal the true face of the dual governmental/military power in Kigali? Groupe Jérémie analyzed this carnage in its April 25 communication.[2]

5. We know that western media reports biased information about the Rwandan tragedy that discredits the refugees. What can you, as groups representing European churches who have their own media outlets, do to pass on objective information which does not distort the Rwandan tragedy? Isn't this now another ethnocide?

We are grateful for your visit and interest in these grave human issues.

---

2. Editor's note: Groupe Jérémie was a civil society group in Bukavu that reported many of the human rights abuses that occurred from 1994 to 1996. Munzihirwa worked closely with the group.

Second Letter to UN Secretary General Boutros Boutros-Ghali (May 15, 1995)

Mr. Secretary General,

Concerning: the problem of the Rwandan refugees in Kivu (Zaire) and the danger of an implosion in the Great Lakes region

As you know, there are a million and a half Rwandan refugees in the Goma and Bukavu regions of Zaire. While the great powers seem to want to support the status quo, or would prefer just to see Zaire integrate these refugees (as the United States of America and Great Britain have said), we are already seeing warning signs of possible clashes and the destabilization of the entire region. These distressing developments have led me to appeal to you directly: it is necessary, it seems to me, that the international bodies interested in the future of the region immediately engage in a serious political examination of the situation in the Great Lakes, and particularly in Rwanda.

1. A WORD ON THE RELATIONSHIP BETWEEN THE LOCAL POPULATION AND THE RWANDAN REFUGEES

1.1 The living conditions for the refugees have become grave: supplies were significantly reduced after the Rwandan government refused to let trucks proceed to Goma and Bukavu. On April 11, the RPF raided the Birava camp near Bukavu, resulting in thirty-seven deaths and sixty serious injuries, creating a sense of anxiety and uncertainty among the refugees. This has improved somewhat with the arrival and presence of Zairian soldiers responsible for security in the camps (CZSC).[1] Under the present conditions,

---

1. Editor's note: CZSC refers to the Zairian Security Contingent for the Camps, a

though, especially after the carnage of Kibeho, those refugees who want to return to Rwanda consider it impossible. Most of them regret the horrible genocide and want reconciliation.

1.2 The people of Zaire, who generously welcomed the refugees, are now showing their concern. If the refugees go hungry, is there not a risk of some of them attacking the local inhabitants, who also live in misery? Moreover, the local population, like the refugees, reject the possibility of an integration, which would create more problems than it would solve in an already overcrowded Kivu (the problem of nationality, conflicts such as those in Bunyakiri, etc.). This is why they are waiting for the conditions, known to everyone, that will allow the refugees to return home.

2. SOME WORDS ON THE EVOLVING SITUATION IN THE REGION

2.1 It is worth noting the interests that now unite the political powers in Rwanda, Burundi, and Uganda, as well as how their armies are collaborating in the abuses suffered by the refugees.

2.2 The divergent interests between the government in Kinshasa and the president of the Republic of Zaire make it difficult to manage the problem and find a solution that is beneficial to the people of Zaire and Rwanda.

2.3 As for those in power in Kigali, which is actually a dual military and governmental power experiencing infighting between various factions, there is a hardline wing that pursues a policy of depopulation. There are countless victims of arbitrary arrests and revenge now crowding prisons or other places of detention. There they die or are kidnapped at night. This then allows for some fifteen hundred to two thousand additional arrests each month. The acts of genocide perpetrated inside Rwanda by the hardline wing in power, most notably the Kibeho massacre, have shown the true face of power in Kigali, and one fears, with the upcoming elections, a further hardening of the extremists in power, in the form of a will to eliminate as much of the Hutu population as possible.

2.4. We've learned that a number of RPF agents are present in Bukavu and Goma, while Rwandan and Zairian insurgents are making incursions into Rwanda.

---

deployment of roughly one thousand Zairian Army soldiers charged with improving security in the refugee camps near Bukavu and Goma.

2.5 Recently, there were several attacks on Lake Kivu by RPF soldiers who killed Zairian fishermen on Zairian territory. Heavy weapons pointed toward Zaire have been installed in Bugarama, Rwanda, and in Nkombo (the island facing Birava). And trucks with goods intended for markets in Zaire were systematically blocked in Rwanda.

2.6. This situation could degenerate into clashes between the Rwandan army (RPA) and the Zairian army; in fact, this already happened for an hour in Panzi on Sunday, March 26. Since then, they have dug trenches along the border. In light of these developments, one fears that the Rwandans will be forced to repatriate, with the complicity of the Zairian army. This could provoke another genocide.

3. THERE IS STILL TIME TO ACT FOR PEACE IN THE REGION

3.1. The solution to this problem will be political, hence my appeal to you for a political analysis of the situation in Rwanda.

3.2. Please carefully consider the following recommendations:

- begin a dialogue with representatives of the Rwandan refugees and the government in Kigali;
- ensure regular and sufficient supplies in the camps;
- find an acceptable solution for the Rwandan Army in exile;
- halt the arms trade which has spread throughout the region;
- issue arrest warrants for the real culprits of genocide and ethnic cleansing, and judge them;
- put an end to the policy of arbitrary arrests, disappearances, assassinations, and depopulation;
- finally, encourage political negotiations and respect for the spirit of Arusha.

This is how we can take into account the desire of the people—on the inside and outside—who reject the military solution and want to reconcile and live in peace.

Please accept, Mr. Secretary General, my highest regards.

Concerning the Forced Repatriation of the Rwandan Refugees (August 24, 1995)

WE HAVE LEARNED THAT after informing the UN and the authorities in Kigali, the Zairian government began expelling the Rwandan refugees. It has conducted several operations, many of them marred by violence. International opinion is stirring. Some parts of the Zairian public approve.

WHAT SHOULD WE THINK?

Zaire has no shortage of reasons to protest. The presence of a million and half refugees in an overpopulated region already weakened by ethnic divisions is an increasingly difficult burden to bear. Kigali's attempts to hinder food aid to the refugees has made the situation even more difficult. Rumors, real or not, of military preparations among the refugees and the incursions of RPF soldiers into the Kivus has further raised tensions. The Zairian population, tired of the interminable democratic transition, fears that the presence of refugees will be used in order to postpone elections forever. The presence of the refugees is a huge burden upon Zaire. The announcement that the arms embargo in Kigali will be lifted only deepens the sense of frustration.

One wonders, however, if the Zairian government could have protested another way. It has had a long time to work with the UN to find solutions and consider possible alternative strategies. Nothing seems to have been seriously entertained. It has simply watched the situation deteriorate. Today, one gets the feeling that certain decisions were made for internal, political reasons. For some state officials, the fate of the refugees seems to be the least of their worries.

Despite their desire to return home, the refugees do not return. Why? They are afraid of dying. They are terrified that the actual perpetrators of the massacres are not distinguished from the mass of people who did nothing wrong. They are flooded with reports, true or false, of what's happening back home. The events of Kibeho confirmed what they heard was happening in many other places. They know that in Rwanda a false denunciation can land someone in prison; they know that those who are imprisoned run the risk of dying before ever being judged. They know that merely returning to their fields, which others now occupy, can result in their denunciation. Zaire took in the refugees to save their lives; can it now force them to repatriate, against their will, at the risk of losing their lives?

UNHCR's mission is to take care of refugees. It should have found more humane solutions for the peaceful and voluntary return of the refugees long ago. Instead, the refugees are slowly left to starve. UNHCR knows the refugees' desire to return home and the reasons that hold them back. It does not seem to have seriously entertained solutions to this dilemma. UNHCR is not unaware of Kivu's problems and knows that the region could not support so many refugees this long. It remains shockingly passive in the face of the crisis.

AND THE CHURCH OF BUKAVU?

She has one law: the gospel's love commandment. She knows that these refugees are human beings like us, our brothers. Christians have done everything possible to welcome the refugees, first the Tutsis, then the Hutus. The Church knows that the presence of refugees weighs heavily upon the population and the current situation demands urgent solutions, but she cannot allow them to be treated like cattle at a slaughterhouse.

The Church of Bukavu is appalled by the callousness of those who decided to force the refugees to return to Rwanda. She notes with great sadness the harshness of those who brutally carry out these measures. She finds that human life has no value in their eyes and that they are only interested in money. She fears that they wouldn't balk at selling their own Zairians like the petty kings of the Atlantic coast did during the slavery era centuries ago.

The Church of Bukavu also notes the growing indifference of foreign states. Perhaps they are tired of supporting this refugee population since the television no longer broadcasts images of their generosity? Individual good will has not been lacking, but governments are becoming increasingly more detached. They seem less and less concerned about the fate of the refugees, as if they had no responsibility for the current situation. Yet many of them know that what has happened can play to their advantage. They seem unconcerned about getting to the truth of the tragic events that caused these misfortunes. Is anyone still looking for the assassins of President Habyarimana? Journalists nonetheless provide astonishing information about the uniforms of those who shot down the plane. The true authors of the genocide sleep in peace while we prey upon those who have been manipulated and victimized. Their justice simply plays into the hands of those who want to maintain the idea that all Hutus are murderers.

The Church of Bukavu observes with astonishment the international media's systematic misrepresentation of this situation. In London or Brussels, there are some who confidently denounce military preparations that no one on the ground has heard anything about. She is shocked by the persistent silence that surrounds the often heroic gestures of protection and solidarity offered on both sides since April 1994. Many of the Tutsi living in Rwanda who escaped the massacres were protected by their Hutu brothers. Even today, there are Tutsis who have found a way to extend friendship to those who fled. The Church thinks that it is important to speak of this as well. This would encourage hope! The Church in Bukavu knows that despair often leads to something worse, but hope can stir things back to life, even where there has been only death.

Letter to the High Commissioner for Refugees (October 6, 1995)

Madam High Commissioner,

Concerning the return of refugees to Rwanda: prelude to peace or war?

The declarations which have followed the various meetings and gatherings of the past few weeks lead one to believe that a good solution to the Rwandan refugee problem in Zaire has been found: they will voluntarily return to their country at the end of the year. It seems to me that this solution risks only bringing about an impasse that will plunge the Great Lakes region into war.

It is a fact that the presence of a million and a half refugees in Kivu has become too great a burden for the inhabitants to bear, and it is possible that it will degenerate into a confrontation between the refugees and the local population. What future do these refugees have when Zaire no longer wants them? Does Rwanda want them?

The Rwandan government says it will accept and welcome them. It asks for money to this end. But in his speeches in Kinyarwanda, the vice-president, General Kagame, expresses disdain for these refugees and insults them. In addition, there has been a political hardening: indeed, the ministers in favor of dialogue have been dismissed. What's more, the refugees have specific reasons to fear going home:

The killings in Kibeho in April left thousands of the displaced dead. A senior UNAMIR official saw a mass grave of 4,054 victims. And in the days and weeks that followed, thousands of those being hunted down died of exhaustion and violence. Their deaths are met with widespread indifference.

Last month in Kanama, Rwanda, the unjustifiable massacre of 111 people during the night, most of whom were women and children—a massacre acknowledged by the authorities—sent a clear message to the refugees: "If you return, this is the fate that awaits you."

Thus the refugees find themselves stuck: Zaire no longer wants them, and Rwanda does not really want them. It has created a new "Palestinian problem" in Central Africa that runs the risk of provoking conflict and confrontation on the borders of Zaire, Rwanda, and Burundi. This becomes especially pronounced when one considers that significant pressure is being exerted on the refugees for their so-called voluntary return, with the alternative being a forced repatriation as early as next month, with the real risk of serious clashes.

The situation is thus explosive. It is urgent. I make a new appeal to you: the true solution to this painful problem can only come from political negotiations between the authorities in Kigali and the many worthy representatives of the refugees who want reconciliation. It is essential that the international community exerts pressure in this specific direction to ensure a safe and dignified return for the refugees. It is just as essential that UNHCR and the WFP—in collaboration with the Zairian national and local authorities—continue their work in the refugee camps in Zaire, as well as the transit camps and (especially) the receiving centers in Rwanda. This is what peace in the region requires.

Please accept, Madam High Commissioner, my kindest regards.

Letter to the Chief of Staff of the Zairian Armed Forces (FAZ), Major General Eluki Monga Aundu (November 6, 1995)

SUBJECT: MEMORANDUM ADDRESSED TO the attention of the Major General, Chief of Staff of the FAZ, on his visit to South Kivu

Mr. General,

On the occasion of your visit to South Kivu, it is my honor to welcome you and wish you a productive stay in this part of the country experiencing enormous challenges, especially regarding the safety of the people and their belongings.

As you know, our region has been hosting hundreds of thousands of Rwandan and Burundian refugees for over a year. Despite this catastrophic socio-economic situation, the population of South Kivu has, on the whole, done everything it can to welcome these refugees from Rwanda and neighboring Burundi.

Unfortunately, certain elements in our armed forces have committed numerous abuses against these refugees, who are our brothers and sisters. Many of them are continually hassled and robbed of their belongings, especially their vehicles.

The local population itself is not spared. The basic principle of the free movement of the people and their belongings has come to mean nothing in the face of the abuses that peaceful citizens suffer.

There are multiple military checkpoints at the ports, airports, and roads. They are often manned by different ranks of soldiers, without any chain of command.

These soldiers demand "tea" from passersby on the ground that they do not receive salaries or enough to live on. It is true that our soldiers are underpaid or not paid at all. But they are not the only ones experiencing this. If we add up all that they have taken from the population, it would exceed what most civil servants earn.

I believe our soldiers need better support. A regular salary would go a long way towards achieving this. But they also need a chain of command, leaders who organize different ranks of soldiers and speak the same language.

I am convinced that our army has values. After all, before the refugees arrived, it was this army, under effective leadership, that protected South Kivu (and the city of Bukavu in particular) from looting and insecurity.

Everyone appreciates the behavior of the Zairian unit that provided security in the camps, although we still condemn the abuses they committed during the forced repatriation operation. Under the right conditions, this army may still surprise many people by its discipline and service to the nation.

To conclude, I want to commend the regional military authorities who recently took steps to provide some relief to our population. Certain roadblocks have been removed, some investigations have been conducted, and insubordinate soldiers have been punished. But this is not enough. It is imperative that military discipline be strengthened, and that soldiers be given enough to live on so they stop harassing the population of South Kivu, which has been devastated by this socio-economic crisis for far too long.

Please accept, General, my highest regards.

Memorandum to Admiral Mavua Mudima, Vice-Minister of Defense (November 10, 1995)

Mr. Minister,

I want to take this opportunity once again to express our sorrows and concerns.

1. OUR SORROWS

The soldiers who were sent to Bukavu to keep order have become a great burden on the impoverished population. Despite our complaints, there are still checkpoints everywhere holding people ransom.

Anyone who travels must pay taxes to the military, or be stripped of everything and be beaten.

Anyone who arrives in Bukavu from Goma or another location must deal with multiple armed groups:

- He must pay the Civil Guard
- He must pay the police
- He must pay SARM[1]
- He must pay customs. How can we have customs for people who are coming from within the country?

If he refuses to pay, he is beaten and his belongings are confiscated. Did we achieve independence for this?

---

1. Editor's note: SARM stands for the Service d'Action et Renseignements Militaires, or the Action and Military Intelligence Service. SARM agents were notorious for their human rights abuses in the region.

2. OUR CONCERNS

There is talk of sending the Rwandans home. Kigali must receive them with dignity as part of any effective solution.

a) We welcomed them here to save them from death. Would it honor our country to send them back to certain death?

b) The refugees know that Rwanda is their home, but do not want to return there to die.

c) In the event that Zaire forces them to go, they want to be sent back together and not in small groups that could be exterminated under the watch of UNHCR.

d) In the event that precautions are not taken, or the camps fall prey to the brutality and plunder of our soldiers, it is the local population that will be killed by the grenades and mines leftover in the camps.

Forty-Three Days before Christmas (November 12, 1995)

BROTHERS AND SISTERS,

In forty-three days, it will be Christmas.
Will there be an atmosphere of peace and joy?
Let us pray that the Son of God,
who humbled himself to save us,
will soften the hearts of political leaders
hardened by pride and selfishness.
May he convert the hearts of those soldiers
who live only for violence and plunder.
In the gospel, there are examples of good soldiers.
We see that Jesus praised them.
The prayer that we recite before communion
comes from the mouth of a good soldier:
> "Lord, I am not worthy to have you come under my roof;
> but only speak the word, and my servant will be healed." (Matt 8:8)

May we prepare for Christmas by loving our brothers,
especially the refugees who are so imperiled.

May we have the words of Jesus in our hearts:
> "Do to others as you would have them do to you" (Luke 6:31).

Letter to the Refugees
(November 18, 1995)

To my brother and sister refugees,

It is in anguish that we begin this season of Advent. This is a time of conversion to the One who is coming, but also a time of torment because of all that stands in our way.

Since we welcomed you, your fate has in a way become our fate. It is the same Christ who suffers in us all. We therefore cannot accept the measures that have been imposed upon you, which violate your human rights, especially your rights as refugees. A refugee cannot be repatriated against his will, especially when he knows that a certain death awaits him at home.

We know this, and we pray that the measures that threaten you will give way to a more humane and Christian process, in keeping with the Gospel: "Do to others as you would have them do to you" (Luke 6:31). May the Spirit of Christ soften the hardened hearts of decision-makers and enlighten those who cannot grasp the complexity of your situation.

At the same time, we must remember that the God who created us without us will not save us without us. These sufferings in exile must be a purification to prepare for a better, more focused, and more united future. It is ethnic and regional division that has plunged your country into blood and fire.

You cannot rebuild Rwanda without firmly looking to the future. God wipes away the sins of a repentant heart; human beings must imitate this. Other countries provide an example: Spain put an end to its civil war; Russia is in the process of moving on from Communism, which produced so many victims. South Africa is confronting the legacy of apartheid while constructing a national community. Why not Rwanda?

We hope that by entering into the dynamic of Christ, we will be able to wish each other a "Merry Christmas" next month, the joy of the Son of God who is born, little by little, in the gash of human history, and who knows he will die on the cross to save the world. It is this profound joy of true hope—that which hopes against all hope—that I wish you now, and which we will foster together in solidarity while awaiting the day of your return to your homeland.

A wise man said, "Weak is the people who accept defeat, who forget they were sent to watch until their hour comes. Because the hour always comes."

Christmas Letter (1995)

And she gave birth to her firstborn son and wrapped him in bands of cloth, and laid him in a manger, because there was no place for them in the inn.

Luke 2:7

1. GOD VISIBLE BEFORE OUR EYES

Christmas is not a birthday, but the celebration
of the mystery of the coming of the Son of God.
In the heart of the night of the world, among the destitute poor
and the divisions of society, "*a child is born unto us.*"

If the birth of a child is a source of hope
for human beings, it is because the child brings
God's gift of renewal,
like a new shoot of a banana tree
which, without violence, emerges from the old one
that has borne fruit and soon falls to the ground.

This newness is given
in every newborn life.

And this is the Christmas that is coming, because God still wants
to draw near to us in our childlike hearts, in our newness.
We are reborn in his Son. Each day his Father says to him:
"*You are my Son, today I have begotten you.*"
Accordingly, the hope we bring to our brothers

will reflect this renewal,
our acceptance that God is born in us,
and we are born in him through the birth of the Child-God.
A Savior was born unto us and is still being born to save us.

But what Savior, what Liberator?
The one who was announced to us by the prophet
and whose environment he describes.
Isaiah tells us about those for whom this birth
will be a great joy:
> "The people who walk in darkness.
> The inhabitants of the dark country.
> Those under the yoke
> or threatened by enemies..."

It is a people who are suffering, impoverished, hunted down,
and disoriented that Isaiah speaks about,
as if the light in the night was only perceptible
to those who could no longer see anything,
who hoped against all hope.

In our country, there is a mass of refugees, expelled from their country,
who want to return there without knowing how!

As for us, sons and daughters of the land,
what oppressions do we not suffer?
To go to the market with a few goods to sell,
how many taxes do we have to pay before,
during, and after the market!
At every corner of the road, men in military uniform
stop and ask us for dollars.
Where are these poor people going to find dollars?
Do soldiers receive their pay in dollars?
We find three, four roadblocks...
Sometimes they rob you of everything you were going to sell
or all that you earned from several months of work.
We see horrible scenes at the beach in Bukavu
and at customs: a tax for the customs officer,
> a tax for the military in every uniform;

a tax for SNIP,[1] a tax for OZACAF,[2]
a tax for the agronomist, etc.
If you have nothing left to give, they'll hit you
with batons and sometimes the bayonet, then throw you in jail.
It's might makes right! What about the rule of law?
It reminds me of the horrible scene that Livingstone observed
in Nyangwe in 1874, when Arab traders shot at the people
to disperse the market and take
ivory and slaves to Zanzibar.

These days, SNIP, the Civil Guard, and the police
all have jails in the city to extort money from the innocent.
And they are our fellow countrymen!
What do they want to do with this country?
When will we enjoy the happiness of independence?
When will the poor feel at home?

2. HIS BIRTH TODAY

All of this can change if we obey the Liberator
who God gives us.
It's not a warrior that God sends,
but his Only Son who, when he became a child in the womb
of the Virgin Mary, assumed the human condition in full,
except for sin.

He lived the condition of the excluded.
No sooner was he born than King Herod forced him to flee to Egypt.
Later, the crowd demands his head.
Jesus will be a Savior in exile, rejected by his nation.
But he took this on freely.
Because he offers us a true liberation,
which is demanding for each of us.
It entails freely welcoming him in the deepest part

---

1. Editor's note: SNIP stands for Service Nationale d'Intelligence et de Protection, or the National Service of Intelligence and Protection.

2. Editor's note: OZACAF stands for Office Zaïrois du Café, or the Zairian Office for Coffee, under the Ministry of Agriculture, which oversaw coffee exports.

of our hearts, so he can illumine our existence.
He is Light from Light, God from God.
He removes the darkness of sin and selfishness.

May those who are in the refugee camps
(fifty million in the world, ten million in Africa)
know that in the concentration camps,
which were far worse, Father Maximilian Kolbe
gave the highest gift of his life to God
in order to save another prisoner.
It was also in exile, at the risk of his life,
that Tobit buried his brothers.

3. NEW BIRTH

When God becomes a child, he knows that he cannot better express himself
than through the weakness of a child.
It is a disarmed love.
This child's gaze brings us back to the childhood of man,
where God keeps saying to us,
as he does to his beloved Son, "Today I have begotten you."
From now on, we cannot truly look at anyone,
without seeing this Child-God hidden in the face of every being,
who wants to be born there too.

So here is Christmas! Soon it will be the year 1996!
In Persia, it is said that when the New Year arrived, the king proclaimed,
"*Here is a new day, part of a new month,
a new year,
we must renew what time has worn out.*"

4. BIRTH OF A WORLD

Let us open our hearts to receive the Child-Jesus
in whom everything is new.
He who came to break down the wall that separates the peoples;
to dispel the thick darkness in our hearts.
In him, there is neither Jew nor Greek, neither free man nor slave,

neither male nor female, but all are children of the same Father,
all sons, one in his only Son,
all united with those who suffer.
Henceforth, no one can appear in the world
without Christ appearing in him and with him.
The entire universe, through the hidden power of this child,
becomes Epiphany, the manifestation and appearance of Christ.
Humanity is no longer a wandering and scattered flock,
but a community of the Sons of God.
Each of my brothers renews for me
the birth of Bethlehem.

Instead of building ideological walls
that separate ethnic groups,
let us build roads and bridges
that encourage and unite us.

Letter to President Jimmy Carter (January 30, 1996)

MR. PRESIDENT,

Regarding: the return of the Rwandan refugees and the massacres in Rwanda

You have undertaken the difficult task of working for peace in the Great Lakes region, and we sincerely thank you. As distressing news continues to reach us from Rwanda, I would like to share with you the current situation in the refugee camps and inside Rwanda.

The refugees in the camps are currently facing a miserable situation. They feel despised, and are in fact despised by many in the media, even though the great majority of them are innocent victims of extremists. Their living conditions are dire. On the one hand, health care is basic and insufficient. UNHCR, for example, refuses to take care of patients suffering from tuberculosis and diabetes. On the other hand, the prospect of a forced repatriation and the gradual closure of the camps has prompted great anxiety and an unwillingness to return because to return on such terms would be a violation of their rights as refugees.

By law, the Rwandan refugees in Zaire must return to Rwanda. And Zaire rightly asks them to return. But how could they do it now without putting their lives in jeopardy? Massacres and disappearances are occurring at an alarming rate in Rwanda. Some Rwandans who recently left the country have alerted the international community.

We know from reliable sources that the Rwandan government has ordered several officers of the Rwandan Patriotic Army (RPA) based in Akagera Park to kidnap people throughout the territory. These disappearances and massacres are aimed specifically at Hutu intellectuals.

LETTER TO PRESIDENT JIMMY CARTER

Prison conditions are abominable and unspeakable, as is known throughout the world; many of those detained have been arrested arbitrarily, including thousands of women and children. Held without trial and overcrowded, prisoners are sometimes forced to stand and some have rotting feet....

Among the Western countries that have given aid, Belgium's contribution of fifty million francs, intended for the reform of the judicial system, was diverted to other purposes, in all likelihood, the purchase of weapons.

Just as others have already done, we call for an international investigation into the massacres taking place in Rwanda: the massacres since October 1990, the detention conditions aimed at ethnic cleansing, the disappearances and massacres.... Is there not a manifest intention to destroy in part the Hutu group, and certainly all of their intellectuals? This is what Burundi did in 1972 and continues today.

In addition, the United States provides significant financial and military aid to Kigali. We know that fifty American instructors helped with the training of Rwandan Patriotic Army soldiers. And as you certainly know, during the night of November 6–7, 1995, it was with American logistical support and equipment that RPA soldiers attacked Hutu peasants living on the island of Iwawa, located in Rwandan territory near Goma. Among the victims of this attack were refugees in Zaire wrongly thought to be planning an attack on Rwanda.

What are we to make of American aid being used for massacres of innocent civilians? How can one justify American support for a political regime that practices a totalitarian form of power—in flagrant violation of the Arusha Accords—imposing terror and organizing massacres? Shouldn't this aid be conditional upon political negotiations in Rwanda and the right of refugees to return home with dignity and safety?

I sincerely thank you for working for peace in the Great Lakes region. This peace requires, in particular:

- the opening of an international investigation into the massacres (considered by some observers acts of genocide, or a "slow motion genocide") taking place in Rwanda;
- it undoubtedly calls for changes to American financial and military aid, conditioned upon respect for each person's right to life;
- it also requires that UNHCR and the WFP take into account the living conditions of the refugees and their anguish in the face of a forced

return; it's a situation that could trigger clashes at the border and with the inhabitants of Kivu;

- finally, peace in Rwanda and the Great Lakes region requires the opening of political negotiations between the authorities in Kigali and representatives of the refugees who want reconciliation.

In the hopes that your efforts will contribute to peace in our region, please accept, Mr. President, my kindest regards.

Letter to the Church (April 12, 1996)

THIS MORNING, APRIL 12, we buried a student, a victim of violence during the looting at the I.S.T.M. campus.[1]

In our region, this is not an isolated incident, but something that happens routinely. It is the law of force:

Whoever has a gun holds up whoever doesn't. A poor mother or father who goes to the market to make ends meet is stripped of everything they have.

Judges pull out all of the legal tricks to cheat the weak, because they can dangle the threat of jail.

The teacher threatens parents who no longer have the means to pay school fees.

At customs, there are eighteen boxes to check just to claim one's goods, and several checkpoints to pass further down the line.

In doing this, what do they intend for this population?

Let all those who want to make a living by oppressing the people of Bukavu—behaving like the nineteenth-century slave-trader Tippu Tip—know that they are Zairians just like us.

When Zaire's children and possessions are despoiled, God will not bless us.

Dear brothers and sisters, let us get back to human, patriotic, and Christian sentiments. The gospel invites all of us to respect the poor, to respect life.

---

1. Editor's note: I.S.T.M (l'Institut Supérieur des Techniques Médicales de Bukavu) is a medical training school in Bukavu.

Letter to the American Ambassador (April 18, 1996)

Mr. Ambassador,

Concerning: the tragic situation of the people of Bukavu

Following our meeting yesterday, I would like to draw your attention to the double tragedy the people of Bukavu are experiencing due to the massive presence of the Rwandan refugees and Zairian armed forces.

1. THE PRESENCE OF THE RWANDAN REFUGEES

We note that the international community effectively endorses the current situation. Some Western governments have decided to provide the Kigali government with financial support, and in some cases, military aid. Moreover, a consensus seems to be emerging among the great powers that the Rwandan refugees could simply integrate into Zaire.

The living conditions of the refugees are deteriorating due to the reduction of their food supplies. Many go to Bukavu looking for assistance, while six hundred young Rwandans are living on the streets. . . . This increases insecurity and is starting to provoke violence.

Zairians are ready for the refugees to leave. As you know, the Bukavu region is overcrowded. And the massive presence of refugees has exacerbated a miserable situation: deforestation, ecological destruction, rising prices. There is growing conflict between Zairians and the refugees, and tensions are heightened following incursions into Rwanda and the response of the RPA (Rwandan Patriotic Army), including the attack on Panzi (on the Rwanda-Zaire border) in early April. These attacks by the RPA resulted in several deaths. In addition, the frequent laying of landmines on the roads leading out of Bukavu has resulted in further deaths and provoked outcry, indignation, and hostility towards the refugees. Zairians, who have shown great hospitality, want the refugees to return home without delay.

Repatriation, but under what conditions? Indeed, Rwanda does not want them to return. How can safe and secure conditions be met when, as we know, the RPF is systemically eliminating Hutu intellectuals?

The International Tribunal in Arusha will rightly judge the Hutu genocidaires. But if Tutsi genocidaires are exempt from this Tribunal, will it not become one-sided, and therefore, a stumbling block to reconciliation?

Continuing the current situation will certainly have disastrous consequences: there is a great risk of seeing war resume in Rwanda and expand across the Great Lakes region.

2. THE PRESENCE OF THE ZAIRIAN ARMED FORCES

The population of Bukavu is experiencing another tragedy: that of the toxic presence of the Zairian soldiers. With so many refugees here, Bukavu has become, it has been said, an operational zone. We have seen a large influx of armed soldiers and confusion in the city.

To meet their basic needs, these underpaid soldiers resort to stealing from the people. We have become daily witnesses to their despicable acts:

- mothers who go to the market to sell what little they have are ransomed of the money they need to survive and pay their children's school fees;
- those who go to the hospital to pay for medical care are robbed of money they have worked so hard to save;
- at night, soldiers in civilian clothes drive taxis and take unsuspecting passengers to various detention centers, holding them hostage until they pay ten or twenty dollars;
- last Thursday, April 11, following a robbery by soldiers in civilian clothing near the ISTM and subsequent exchanges between students and soldiers, a third-year Tembo student was shot dead by a civilian guard.

Stealing for themselves, these soldiers must also bring a required percentage to their superiors. One wonders if those supporting this situation want to stir the people to revolt, which would then allow the armed forces to pillage all that we have tried to save in the city of Bukavu.

3. RECOMMENDATIONS

Given the gravity of the situation and the tragedy that the people are enduring, I urge you, Mr. Ambassador, to take active steps to safeguard peace in the region.

- It is the historic responsibility of countries such as yours to help facilitate negotiations for a safe and dignified return of the refugees.
- Would it not be possible for you to use your influence with the Zairian authorities, in concert with other parties, to put an end to this tragic situation created by the presence of the refugees and armed forces?
- Please also inform the president and government of the United States of America about the tragedy that the people of Bukavu are experiencing due to the soldiers, the explosive situation in the Great Lakes, and the chronic inconsistency of the Zairian government.

With gratitude for what you can do for peace in the region, please accept, Mr. Ambassador, my kindest regards.

Strength in Unity (September 27, 1996)

DEAR BROTHERS,

1. We have always affirmed our desire for peace with everyone. Unfortunately, in recent days, we have been attacked by soldiers from Rwanda. We deplore the incursion of armed men into the Ruzizi Plain. We also know that cars traveling along the Nkomo road are still being shot at from Rwanda.

2. We can only condemn these acts of provocation and aggression. But at the same time, we have to think about how to defend our homes and country as good patriots. Let us be courageous and vigilant. Our fathers always defended this Bushi region against external aggression; once, all of the ethnic groups united to repel the Mulele Mayi.[1] Yesterday, thanks to your solidarity, you were able to avoid looting. Together, we can rebuild this city and country again.

3. Such courage demands great solidarity and discipline. Our fathers never tried to stoke hatred, enmity, or revenge. When war was over and the peace concluded, former enemies interacted in the same market. From time to time there was also intermarriage. Let us not fall prey to certain refugees who want to bring disorder here. Let UNHCR and our political authorities increase their efforts to monitor young people who roam the city day and night.

4. Let us remain welcoming to everyone, so that we can be enriched by the many values that different ethnicities and races bring. The strongest nations are those that have managed to reconcile their differences. It is foolish to attack peaceful people simply because they belong to

---

1. Editor's note: Munzihirwa is referring to Peter Mulele's unsuccessful rebellion that took place in the Kwilu Province from 1962 to 1965.

this or that ethnic group. None of us chooses our parents or ethnicity. We accept them and defend them.

5. It is wrong to want to take advantage of this state of confusion, to steal from or loot one's neighbor, to harass mixed couples just because they are mixed. To do this is to go against humanity and the will of God, who creates different people and asks them to unite their efforts to creation a more harmonious world.

6. The month of October is called the "month of the rosary." The Church remembers the victory over the Turks at Lepanto on October 7, 1571. On that day, while valiant soldiers defended the homeland and their faith, other members of the faithful prayed the rosary. May the Queen of Peace come to our assistance.

South Kivu Is Attacked by Rwanda Today (October 11, 1996)

WHAT IS THE AIM of Rwanda's repeated attacks in Eastern Zaire?

Rwanda has recently increased its armed attacks against Eastern Zaire. These attacks have already resulted in a number of civilian casualties in Kivu.

Initially it was the refugees who were targeted. We all remember the automatic weapon fire on the Birava camp in South Kivu in April 1995. The result: forty-five dead and more than one hundred injured, mostly women and children. We have not forgotten the RPA's repeated attacks against the camps on the island of Idjwi and in Panzi, near Bukavu.

Anti-personnel or anti-tank mines are continually placed on trade routes in the vicinity of Bukavu and Goma. The frequent explosion of these mines causes human devastation across South and North Kivu.

Today, Rwanda's attacks against South Kivu are intensifying. On September 22, 23, and 24, the city of Bukavu was violently attacked by heavy weapons from Rwanda. There were reports of lives lost and damage to buildings.

Traders driving on the Nkomo road continue to come under fire from Rwandan army positions across the Ruzizi river. As a result, the Uvira area has been cut off from the city of Bukavu.

The island of Idjwi and the fishermen of Lake Kivu have to worry every day about RPA patrols, who shoot at anything that moves.

PART III | THE RWANDAN REFUGEE CRISIS

Skirmishes between armed Tutsi groups from Rwanda and the Zairian army are currently happening in Uvira, Mwenga, Fizi, and Walungu. Some claim (but this has not yet been verified) that Ugandan elements are fighting alongside the Rwandan-trained forces.

The aforementioned armed groups are made up of individuals who lived in Zaire as refugees or as transplants who today are called "Banyamulenge," "Kinyarwanda-speaking Zairians," etc. They recently helped the RPF take power by force in Rwanda.

Now they are killing Zairians and destroying infrastructure in the areas where fighting is occurring. We just learned that they massacred two priests in the Kidote parish of the diocese of Uvira on Sunday, October 6, after pillaging the parish facilities. They also reportedly destroyed and looted the Lemera rural hospital.

Earlier the Zairian authorities announced that attackers executed more than thirty-five people in the mountains of Uvira and certainly many more in the Fizi area.

But what does Kigali want by organizing attacks against Zaire from its territory, going as far as sending members of its own army to wage war in Zaire?

1. Does the Kigali government want to further delay, if not permanently jeopardize, the repatriation of the refugees? To this day, there are still more than one million Rwandan refugees on Zairian soil. As we have repeatedly said, the Kigali government does not want these refugees. Indeed, each time there is a question of repatriation, the Kigali government pushes in the opposite direction: it makes arrests, takes away property, conducts assassinations, arranges dismissals, and generally prevents anyone who is from the majority ethnic group from influencing the Rwandan political scene.

This does not prevent the leaders in Kigali from taking advantage of the attention they receive from certain media and international organizations to release false information. They declare they are ready to welcome all the refugees without any conditions. They accuse the countries who have welcomed these refugees, especially Zaire, of getting in the way of their return to Rwanda; they see bullies everywhere; they treat all the refugees as genocidaires.... None of this encourages the refugees to return to Rwanda. Zaire, however, wants the refugees to return at all costs. Kigali therefore dreams of pulling off a coup: pitting the refugees and their hosts against one another, which will provoke deadly clashes that play right into the hands of the Rwandan authorities.

2. Would Kigali fear a likely war inside Rwanda? There have been frequent reports in recent days of infiltrations by ex-FAR soldiers into Rwanda, and Zaire is accused of supporting them. Couldn't all of this be avoided if the government in Kigali stopped refusing to dialogue with the refugees?

3. Do the leaders of Kigali have imperial ambitions? Is there not support for this by certain neighboring countries and Western powers?

In fact, the powers which claim to promote democracy are only using the geographical position of Rwanda and the minority which governs this small country to establish control over the political, economic, and strategic future of the giant that is Zaire, and possibly other countries in the Great Lakes region.

This attitude of Rwanda and its allies is extremely dangerous:

- It will bring terrible human costs in our region, and Rwanda itself will not be spared.
- It will only serve to isolate Rwanda by stirring up the animosity of other ethnic groups in the region against them.
- Doesn't this expansionist project in turn have genocidal tendencies?

We call upon all nations and states who love justice and human rights to work for peace and security in this region by sparing its inhabitants from the disaster that threatens them.

In closing, we recall that war is always something horrible.
May those who love this region work to build structures of justice, reconciliation, forgiveness, and peace.

Open Letter (October 13, 1996)

Dear beloved,

Let's come together and unite our hearts in cooperation to save our country.

1. Today, as in the past, it is the unity of our hearts and actions that will save Bukavu. We have just experienced the panic caused by the violence from Rwanda and the soldiers who fled the fighting in order to pillage Bukavu.

2. We commend you for your solidarity, mutual support, and conduct, which has discouraged the looting. We also commend the Bukavu police for their efforts. They erected barriers to prevent the deserting soldiers from continuing their abuses. These soldiers fired on the very hospital that welcomed and cared for their wounded. Who are they? They are unsupervised youth from towns and cities who were picked up and integrated into the army. Their aim is not to defend the people but bring home spoils for which they did not fight. Those who came to loot Bukavu fled the combat zone. After fighting and pushing back the enemy, they went back to the villages to sleep, without monitoring the roads. They were bypassed just as Schramme bypassed our soldiers in 1967 via the Kabare-Cidaho road. While our soldiers were stationed along the lake, they discovered that the enemy was already in the city.

3. We call upon the youth of Bukavu to stop roaming the streets and inciting their neighbors to loot. They should instead work together to prevent armed thieves from preying upon the population at night. Know that war still threatens us.

- Do you know that four months ago Uganda, Rwanda, and Burundi organized seven thousand men of war to come destroy the refugee camps from Uvira to Bukavu and Goma?
- Do you know that even now armored vehicles are parked on the Ruzizi Plain, facing the Bujumbura airport? They are waiting for the right moment to invade our country when Zairians might not be looking!
- Do you know that in order to strengthen its army, Burundi organizes a compulsory military service for all youth when they finish secondary school?
- Do you know that spies from Itombwe crossed Bushi the day before yesterday?

What should we do in the face of these threats?

We must be aware of the present danger, of unjust and hostile intentions, and ward them off through prayer and dialogue. Let us never take it out on the innocent among us. We must say never to racism or genocidal intentions! Everyone is innocent until proven guilty.

It is better to prevent war than to wage it.

May Our Lady of Victory come to our aid as she came to the aid of the Church threatened in 629 by a lawless group called the Avors. It was then that a hymn of thanksgiving was composed for "Our Lady of Peace." May she come to us as she came to the aid of Christians against the Turks in 1571. It was in thanksgiving for this occasion that the month of October became the "month of the rosary."

Our Lady of Victory, pray for us!

The University of Bukavu and Peace (October 19, 1996)

TODAY, WHEN WE SPEAK of a university, we think first and foremost of the body of knowledge that it provides. At its origin, around 1230, the university was conceived as a community of students and teachers coming together from all nations to receive instruction. It was a vision of dialogue across ethnicities that informed its sense of universality. Bukavu must get back to this idea. Our happiness will be found in all the different ethnic groups of the Great Lakes coming together as brothers, enriching one another through their differences and ongoing dialogue.

The greatness of a university, like a nation, comes in knowing how to deal with differences instead of destroying them. This is what drives the spirit of innovation and creativity. We must not forget, however, that the fruitfulness of the spirit requires a lasting peace. A proverb says: "*Na fe ahinga, ci nabunge arhahinga*," "he who knows that he will die stays in one place and works, but the person who thinks little of death constantly moves around and has little dedication to work."

Saint Augustine defined peace as "the tranquility of order." In antiquity, the *pax Romana* enabled an expansion of culture and science. When Christianity spread in the Middle Ages, universities began to take off. Today, the European peace promotes education and all of the opportunities that come with it.

Can we still develop a university in Liberia? Who today would pursue studies in Burundi? And if we are not careful, who will continue to send their children to study in Kivu? Are we not in fact seeing the opposite tendency, that those looking for education are increasingly taking their families outside Kivu?

Today we confer degrees to our graduates in economics. Will they be willing to work if they are constantly threatened with bullets from Rwanda or Burundi, if their savings are confiscated by soldiers run amok?

THE ROLE OF INTELLECTUALS

We know that while the great European intellectuals did not succeed in preventing the war of 1939 to 1946, their collaborative thinking did succeed in founding, after the war, a society based upon peaceful and constructive competition, rather than destructive and hostile competition.

The result of this peaceful and constructive competition is the peace we have known in the European Union for fifty years now. And with this peace we can point to the respect for human rights, the defense and protection of basic freedoms that ensure a certain dignity for every human being.

To achieve such dignity, education is the essential condition. Education is not only the search for truth, but also the struggle against ignorance. In his *Dialogue with Trypho*, Saint Justin observes that the devil tempts us first by confusing our minds, so that when people are misled by their ignorance, the devil can realize his malicious ends through false logic and empty pleasures.

We also know how ignorance is the mother of all vice, and that dictatorial regimes set out to subdue whole peoples through blatant terror and injustice.

Let us therefore make the struggle against ignorance our battle cry, and collaboration with all peoples our tactic for achieving peace and prosperity. Work, when it is rooted in collaboration and transparent management, is the key to prosperity. Postwar Germany has become what it is now thanks to such collaboration and management.

The Marshall Plan, set up by a great American by that name, rejected the impulse for revenge that would have destroyed what remained of Germany after WWII. Is it not possible for the Americans, Germans, Belgians, and French to make a similar investment for peace in a socially reconciled Rwanda and Burundi, instead of developing a war machine that keeps the arms trade going and victimizes Kivu simply because we have extended hospitality to a mass of people who were excluded from their homeland?

Their stay here is not only a humanitarian emergency, but also, on several levels, an ecological disaster the consequences of which the Kivu population unfortunately bears painfully alone, along with the other indignities, to say nothing of the social and political costs. One fears their presence here will bring about not only their death but also our own. Can we not, instead, work together to ensure their peaceful return?

I would like to end by urging our students not to get caught up in violence and ethnic division. It is the harmonious coexistence of difference that develops the world and not the other way around. Any ethnic cleansing is a crime against humanity and a grave mistake.

Rabelais wrote that wisdom does not enter a bad soul, and that science without conscience ruins the soul.

Run to the summits of unity, and do not descend the slopes of degradation.

We need peace in order to develop. Not the peace of armies who are always on a war footing, or the peace of the cemetery, but the living and invigorating peace that allows us to develop the economic, legal, agricultural, and medical sciences of our university.

We need to develop research that is rooted in the soil and prevents erosion. We need agricultural research that not only helps us improve plant and animal species, but also enables us to restore a sense of ecological balance by reforesting our barren hills, which have been destroyed through ignorance of the negative consequences of deforestation, or worse, the greedy short-sightedness of those who have only sought to enrich themselves without realizing that they are exposing others to deadly erosion.

We need medical research in preventive, nutritional, and curative medicine. If we understand that a healthy diet is the first medication, we will also understand the importance of a certain interdisciplinarity in our university. Let doctors and researchers promote the cultivation and protection of medicinal plants, and deepen our knowledge of the beneficial effects of certain plants for life and harmonious growth. May they also recall the great sense of respect for the human person contained in the Hippocratic Oath. And may this sense of respect for the human person also be reflected in our study of the law, so that we can finally realize the beneficial effects of principles of sound management and national prosperity.

To the economists, I would say that the economy, far from being merely a matter of numbers and interests, is above all governed by ethics. This means knowing that a good economist does not steal or enrich himself through dishonest means, but rather seeks to earn the trust of his clients. This trust reflects the quality of the services he offers. In the same vein, we will need to instill in parents who engage in trade the meaning of sound and careful management, forecasting and asset management, and other laws of political economy or commercial policy that we have learned here at the university.

If we avoid what in economics is called "unbridled liberalism," and instead contribute to a humane liberalism that serves Man and Society, we will have accomplished our mission. Business ethics is the ethics of justice and fairness. And fairness, which involves a capacity for discernment, will enable us to hope for sound management and national prosperity.

The experience of Zaire teaches us that sound management is rooted in ethics. Without ethics, the economy falls into ruin.

In appealing to national prosperity, I would like to remind you of the collaboration between ethnic groups that I mentioned at the beginning of my remarks and which seems to me to be the only way to promote peace and fraternity, the principle and end of university education.

The peace we wish to promote must come from the recognition that every human being is a child of God, a brother and sister of Christ (Rom 8:29).

May the God who is peace dwell in our hearts.

Remain Strong in Love (October 27, 1996)

To priests and vicars

Dear all,

Remain strong in your parishes. Do not let yourselves be misled by foreign radio stations, which are funded by those who support the Rwandan government. It is through them that the RPF seeks to intoxicate the population and sow panic.

Also, do not let yourself be intoxicated by soldiers who have not been on the frontlines or seen the enemy. Those who have been on the frontlines have more inspiring stories to share. They have bravely defended the nation and should be recognized for their bravery. During these difficult times, they deserve encouragement, which we can show by maintaining a sense of peace and calm.

On the other hand, there are soldiers who have fled the fighting; they have come to pillage rather than defend the country. They tell incredible stories to sow panic among people in the hopes of driving them away, so they can steal and plunder more easily.

Let our journalists seize this opportunity to offer those who are here, and the rest of the world, more objective news, which, in keeping with their moral duty, can give people a true sense of the facts. This will help mitigate the unjustified panic that the RPF, one the one hand, and those who have fled the fighting, on the other, are trying to sow. I would like to remind these soldiers who are only strong in front of unarmed civilians to stop harassing us. Let them go to the front, where real soldiers belong.

Let us therefore stay at home and encourage our valiant soldiers not to abandon the city of Bukavu or the country into the hands of the enemy. Let us unite to save the nation.

- In 1964, cowardly soldiers ran from Mulelists who said they were invincible and invulnerable. These kinds of stories are beautiful and good for Zairian literature. When the provincial government took up arms alongside Colonel Mulamba and some brave soldiers, Kabare, Ngweshe, and Lungangi had already alerted the population, so as not to allow the rebels to enter their homes. This part of our history should serve as an example. Let's not let the enemy into our homes. Let's not give them free access by fleeing our city. And do not listen to all those who, from afar, spread lies to sow panic and division.
- We will not allow young people under the influence of drugs to be set loose in the city to menace the population or betray them during the fighting.

As we go about our daily business, let us be on the watch for any suspicious activity. Let's keep the military and those who are responsible apprised of such activity so that, if necessary, they can investigate it.

We Christians know that our greatest weapon is love towards everyone and prayer to Christ through our Lady of the Rosary. May the Virgin Mary, Queen of Peace and our Mother, intercede for us.

Bibliography

Allen, Elise Ann. "Pope Extols 'Romero of Africa' as Role Model for Congo's Bishops." *Crux*, Feb 3, 2023. https://cruxnow.com/pope-in-south-sudan-congo/2023/02/pope-extols-romero-of-africa-as-role-model-for-congos-bishops.

Allen, John Jr. "Sixteen Years Ago Today, Death Came for the Archbishop." *National Catholic Reporter*, Oct 29, 2012. https://www.ncronline.org/blogs/ncr-today/sixteen-years-ago-today-death-came-archbishop.

Amoussou, Luc Bonaventure A. "Munzihirwa, Christophe, S.J." In *The Cambridge Encyclopedia of the Jesuits*, edited by Thomas Worcester, 533–34. Cambridge: Cambridge University Press, 2017.

Chatelain, Daniel, and Pierre Tafani. *Qu'est-ce qui fait courir ces autonomistes?* Paris: Stock, 1976.

Cnockaert, André, ed. *In Memoriam: Monseigneur Christophe Munzihirwa, S.J. Serviteur et Témoin*. Bukavu: Loyola, 1997.

Coghlan, Benjamin, et al. "Mortality in the Democratic Republic of Congo: A Nationwide Survey." *Lancet* 367 (2006) 44–51.

Dalla Zuanna, Gianpiero. "Social Mobility and Fertility." *Demographic Research* 17 (2007) 441–64.

de Dorlodot, Philippe. "L'engagement politique de Mgr Christophe Munzihirwa 1926–1996." In *Mission et engagement politique après 1945: Afrique, Amérique latine, Europe*, edited by Caroline Sappia and Olivier Servais, 333–42. Paris: Karthala, 2009.

———, ed. *Les réfugiés rwandais à Bukavu au Zaïre: De nouveaux Palestiniens?* Paris: L'Harmattan, 1996.

de Haes, René. *Les sects: Une interpellation*. Kinshasa: St. Paul Afrique, 1982.

Dia, Mamadou. *Nations africaines et solidarité mondiale*. Paris: Presses Universitaires de France, 1960.

Edighoffer, Roland. *Les Rose-Croix*. Paris: Presses Universitaires de France, 1986.

Ericson, Edward E., Jr., and Daniel J. Mahoney, eds. *The Solzhenitsyn Reader: New and Essential Writings, 1947–2005*. Wilmington, DE: ISI Books, 2006.

Francis. "Address of His Holiness Pope Francis to the Episcopal Conference of the Congo (CENCO)." https://press.vatican.va/content/salastampa/en/bollettino/pubblico/2023/02/03/230203c.html.

Fustel de Coulanges, Numa Denis. *L'Alsace: Est-elle Allemande ou Française?* Paris: E. Dentu, 1870.

George, Susan. *Comment meurt l'autre moitié du monde*. Paris: Robert Laffont, 1978.

Grand-Maison, Jacques. "Le parti liberal de la Cöte-d'Ivoire." *Masses Ouvrières* 327 (1976) 2–12.

———. "Tanzanie, un nouveau socialism africain?" *Masses Ouvrières* 328 (1976) 3–14.

Kataliko, Emmanuel. "Console, Console My People: Hope Never Disappoints." In *Lettres Pastorales et Messages de Monseigneur Emmanuel Kataliko*. Bukavu: Archevêché, 2000.

Katongole, Emmanuel. "Christopher Munzihirwa and the Politics of Nonviolent Love." In *Born from Lament: The Theology and Politics of Hope in Africa*, 164–78. Grand Rapids, MI: Eerdmans, 2017.

Kitumaini, Jean-Marie Vianney. "L'agir socio-politique de Mgr Christophe Munzihirwa à Bukavu (1994–1996, R.D. Congo)." *Nouvelle revue théologique* 126 (2004) 204–17.

———. *Nouveaux enjeux de l'agir socio-politique de l'Eglise face aux défis de la société en Afrique*. Paris: L'Harmattan, 2011.

Kohn, Hans. *L'idée du nationalism*. Paris: Presses Universitaires de France, 1968.

Kyungu, Rigobert Musenge. *La liberté interieure comme fruit du discernement spirituel: Tentative d'un portrait spirituel du Serviteur de Dieu Monseigneur Christophe Munzhirwa, S.J., Archevêque de Bukavu (1926–1996)*. Kinshasa: Loyola, 2020.

Lacroix, Jean. *Le sens du dialogue*. Neuchatel: de la Baconnière, 1962.

Lock, Gauthier Malulu. *Mgr Christophe Munzihirwa: Exercises Spirituels d'Ignace de Loyola et l'engagement social chrétien*. Saarbrücken: Éditions universitaires européennes, 2016.

———. "Un profil spirituel de Mgr Christophe Munzhirwa Mwene Ngabu." *Nouvelle revue théologique* 129 (2007) 620–25.

Marchesi, Giovanni, and Jean-Marie Vianney Kitumaini, eds. *Christophe Munzihirwa: Lettere et appelli dal Congo*. Bologna: EMI, 2007.

Marx, Karl. "Draft of an Article on Friedrich List's book *Das Nationale System der Politischen Oekonomie*." In *Collected Works*, edited by Karl Marx and Friedrich Engels, 265–93. Vol. 4. London: Lawrence and Wishard, 1975.

Maus, Marcel. "La nation." *L'Année sociologique* 3 (1954) 7–68.

Mayer, Jean-François. *Sectes Nouvelles*. Paris: du Cerf, 1985.

Mirindi Ya Nacironge, Deogratias. *Père Evêque Christophe Munzihirwa Mwene Ngabo, S.J.: Prophète et martyr en notre temps*. Bukavu: Centre Interdiocésain de Pastorale, Catéchèse et Liturgie, 2003.

Mukabalera, J. Cigirwa. "Monseigneur Christophe Munzihirwa, Romero du Congo? Les Concepts de Martyr, de Béatification et de Canonisation revisités à la Lumiere de l'histoire religeuse contempororaire de la martyrologie et de l'expérience pastorale de Monseigneur Christophe Munzihirwa, Archevêche de Bukavu." PhD diss., Université Libre de Bruxelles, 2004.

Mukwege, Denis. "The Role of the Church in the Pathway to Peace." YouTube video, August 20, 2016. youtube.com/watch?v=qpmWyoa1Gr8.

Mulombe, Sébastien Muyengo. *Christophe Munzihirwa: La sentinelle des Grands Lacs*. Kinshasa: Afriquespoir, 2011.

Munzihirwa, Christophe. "Pouvoir royal et ideologies: Role du mythe, des rites et des proverbs dans la monarchie précoloniale du royaume de Kabaré (Zaïre)." *Journal des africanistes* 72:1 (2002) 227–61.

Nzongola-Ntalaja, Georges. *The Congo: From Leopold to Kabila*. London: Zed Books, 2002.

BIBLIOGRAPHY

Okitembo, Louis Ngomo. *L'engagement politique de l'Église catholique au Zaïre, 1960–1992.* Paris: L'Harmattan, 1998.

Oyatambwe, Wamu. *Eglise catholique et pouvoir politique au Congo-Zaïre: La quête démocratique.* Paris: L'Harmattan, 1997.

Prunier, Gérard. *Africa's World War: Congo, the Rwandan Genocide, and the Making of a Continental Catastrophe.* Oxford: Oxford University Press, 2011.

———. "The Catholic Church and the Kivu Conflict." *Journal of Religion in Africa* 31:2 (2001) 139–62.

Renan, Ernest. *Qu'est-ce qu'une nation?* Paris: Calman Lévy, 1882.

Renton, David, et al. *The Congo: Plunder and Resistance.* London: Zed Books, 2007.

Retzius, Gustav, and Carl M. Fürst. *Anthropologia Suecica: Beiträge zur Anthropologie der Schweden.* Stockholm: Aftonbladets Druckerei, 1902.

Sachs, Ignacy. *Pour une economie politique du développement.* Paris: Flammarion, 1977.

Safi Turner, Irene. "Mgr. Christophe Munzihirwa: Leadership and Influence on the Dynamics of the Congo Conflict." PhD diss., George Mason University, Virginia, 2018.

Sauvy, Alfred. *La fin des riches.* Paris: Calmann-Lévy, 1975.

Senghor, Léopold Sédar. *Nation et voie africaine du socialism.* Paris: Présence Africaine, 1959.

Stearns, Jason K. *Dancing in the Glory of Monsters: The Collapse of the Congo and the Great War of Africa.* New York: PublicAffairs, 2011.

United Nations Human Rights Office of the High Commissioner. *Report of the Mapping Exercise Documenting the Most Serious Violations of Human Rights and International Humanitarian Law Committed Within the Territory of the Democratic Republic of the Congo between March 1993 and June 2003.* August 2010.

Vergnaud, Pierre. *L'idée de la nationalité et de la libre disposition des peoples.* Paris: Donat-Montchrestien, 1955.

Vernette, Jean. *Jésus dans la nouvelle religiosité.* Paris: Desclée, 1987.

———. *Sectes et réveil-religieux.* Mulhouse: Salvator, 1976.

Yamb, Gervais. "L'Afrique d'Engelbert Mveng et de Christophe Munzihirwa: Essai de lecture et de thématisation," *Telema 100* (1999) 64–73.

Young, Crawford, and Thomas Turner. *The Rise and Decline of the Zairian State.* Madison: University of Wisconsin Press, 1985.

Index

AFDL (Alliance des Forces Démocratiques pour la Libèration), 23–26
Alexander the Great, 131, 132
Amos, 119
Angola, 122
Antigone, 109
Aristotle, 63–64
arms trade, 21, 122, 125, 147, 150, 151, 183
Arrupe, Pedro, SJ, 5
Arusha Accords, 150, 169
l'Athénée d'Ibanda, 96
Augustine, Saint, 16n57, 87, 93, 94, 124, 131, 182
Aundu, Eluki Monga, Major General, 156–57
authenticité, 6–8, 10, 56, 60, 77, 80

Bakanja, Isidore, Saint, 13, 100–102
Banyamulenge, 22, 178
baraza, 66
Bashi, 3, 5, 85, 86
Belgium, 5, 6, 47, 48, 143, 169
Berdyaev, Nikolai, 70
Birava refugee camp, 144, 147, 148, 177
Bismarck, Otto von, 46
Bonhoeffer, Dietrich, 27
Boutros-Ghali, Boutrous, 121, 148–50
Bro, Bernard, OP, 108
Bukavu
    Archdiocese of, 1, 17, 100–103, 121, 142, 152–53, 171
    city of, 5, 17, 18, 22, 23, 24, 95–96, 98, 99, 103, 117, 119, 121, 124, 128–29, 130, 132–33, 135, 140, 144–45, 146, 148, 149, 157, 158, 164, 177, 180–81, 186
    people of, 3, 14, 132, 147n2, 171, 172–74, 180
    University of, 15–16, 182–85
Burundi, 5, 20, 123, 124, 126, 127, 140, 144, 145, 149, 155, 156, 169, 181, 182–83
Bushi region, 20, 129, 135, 137, 175, 181

Caritas International, 128, 146
Carter, Jimmy, 21n81, 168–70
Catholic Church, 58, 86, 100–101, 105, 107, 138, 141, 176, 181
    and Belgian colonialism, 6
    in Democratic Republic of the Congo, 2, 6, 96, 124–25, 127, 152–53, 160, 161–62, 167, 171, 175–76, 180–81, 186–87
    in Europe, 48, 143, 147
    in Great Lakes region, 122–27
    peacebuilding role of, 3, 88–89, 124–25, 127, 145
    prophetic role of, 2, 8, 18, 27, 127, 152–53
    status under Mobutu regime, 2, 4, 6–7, 96
    See also authenticité; Bukavu, Archdiocese of; Rwandan refugee crisis
Catholic Social Teaching, 2, 12. *See also Gaudium et Spes.*
CCAC (Concertation Chrétienne pour l'Afrique Centrale), 146–47

193

INDEX

Christmas, 13, 19–20, 26, 104–7, 160, 162, 163–67
College Alfajiri, 24, 128
colonialism, 6, 8, 37, 43, 52, 54, 64, 66, 75, 131. *See also* neocolonialism.
common good, 8, 22, 45, 49, 56, 58, 59, 63, 65, 70, 97, 125
conscience, 4, 11, 15, 58–59, 90, 96–99, 140, 184
    Christian, 8, 14, 18, 60, 96, 117–18, 119, 126
Cornelius, 139
corruption, 2, 6, 7, 65, 71, 80, 92, 96, 118, 134
Côte d'Ivoire, 37, 40
crimes against humanity, 119, 121, 143, 184
cross, 12–13, 70, 83–85, 87–89, 93–94, 106–7, 124, 162
culture
    African 2, 3, 6, 7, 9, 33, 40, 52–53, 76–77, 125, 140
    and education 46, 59, 182
    and nationhood 48–50
    and nature 15, 61, 96
    of truth 10, 23
    See also enculturation
Cyrus, 106
CZSC (Contingent Zairois de la Sécurité des Camps), 148

Danneels, Godfried, Cardinal, 142–43, 147
de Dorlodot, Philippe, 124
death, 9, 16, 24–25, 32–34, 41, 85, 88–89, 93–94, 107, 109–10, 153, 159, 161, 182, 184
Delaporte, Jacques, Mgr., 142–43, 147
decolonization, 1, 3, 43, 64–65, 75
democracy, 1, 2, 10–11, 37, 41, 63–74, 77–80, 123, 125, 126, 136, 143, 179
    African roots of, 66–67, 78–80
    democratization movement in Zaire/Congo, 1, 2, 6, 10, 75–80, 109
    in ancient Greece, 65–66, 77–78
    emergence in Europe, 67

Democratic Republic of the Congo
    civil society, 11, 23, 180–81
    democratization, 1, 2, 6, 10, 75–80, 109
    independence, 6
    relationship with Rwanda, 17, 18, 20–21, 22–23, 25–26, 102, 123, 126, 128, 130–31, 136, 142–45, 149–50, 152, 154–55, 159, 168–70, 172–73, 175–81, 186
    military abuses, 18, 21–22, 26, 95–96, 103, 117–19, 132–33, 156–59, 173–74, 180, 186
    Mobutu regime, 6–10, 15, 18, 25, 56, 80, 96, 117, 129, 145, 149, 151
    war in, 3, 25–26, 175–81, 186–87
    See also Catholic Church; FAZ; Mobutu, Joseph-Désiré; Rwandan refugee crisis
development, 1, 2, 9, 11, 31–42, 52–54, 55–62, 67, 92
Dia, Mamadou, 52
dictatorship, 2, 7, 10, 46, 64–65, 67, 70, 72, 98, 120, 125
discernment, 2, 16, 84, 185
discipleship, 1, 2, 12–17, 18, 83–94, 100, 113–14, 127
Dismas, 93
Dostoevsky, Fyodor, 34, 58

Easter, 14, 85–91, 94
education, 2, 15–16, 36–37, 45–46, 50, 53, 59, 64, 78, 97–98, 173, 182–85
enculturation, 1, 2, 3, 5, 7–9, 56, 91, 125
equality, 10, 35, 36, 39, 50, 52, 64, 68, 72–74, 77–78, 88
ethnic cleansing, 150, 169, 184
ethnic conflict, 16, 23, 64, 102, 122–27, 151, 161, 175, 179, 181, 184
ethnicity, 47–50, 103, 167, 176, 182

faith, 15, 26, 59–61, 71, 86, 89, 91, 93, 96, 101, 113, 125, 133, 138, 176
family, 2, 15–16, 32–33, 58–59, 89–90, 95–99, 100–102
FAR (Forces Armées Rwandaises), 179

INDEX

FAZ (Forces Armées Zaïroises), 18, 21–22, 95–96, 103, 117–18, 119, 132, 156–59, 173–74, 180, 186
Felicity, Saint, 13, 110
forgiveness, 15, 76n1, 88, 93, 99, 120, 124–25, 145, 179
France, 46, 47, 120, 140, 143, 183
French (nationality/culture), 51, 71
Francis, Pope, 27
fraternity, 37, 50, 72, 73, 77–78, 185
freedom, 10, 22, 31, 34–35, 50, 52, 58–59, 60, 64, 67–69, 72–74, 77–78, 79, 90, 91, 97, 98, 125, 140, 143, 156
French Revolution, 44, 50, 56
Freud, Sigmund, 31
Fustel de Coulanges, Numa Denis, 47

Gaudium et Spes, 22, 90, 133, 139–40
genocide, 17, 23, 122, 126, 145, 147, 149–50, 153, 169, 181. *See also* Rwandan genocide.
George, Saint, 141
George, Susan, 38
Germany, 43, 44, 46, 47, 126, 183
German (nationality/culture), 51, 126
Gethsemane, 14, 87, 93, 94
God, 2, 12–13, 19–20, 24–25, 27, 33, 41, 50, 53, 57–61, 70–71, 78, 83–84, 86–90, 92, 94, 95, 97, 100–103, 104–7, 108, 110, 112, 114, 124, 130, 134, 138–39, 141, 160, 161–62, 163–67, 171, 176, 185
Goma, 17, 22, 148–49, 158, 169, 177, 181
Good Friday, 14, 93–94
Great Britain, 48, 120, 148
English (nationality/culture), 37, 43, 48, 51
Groupe Jérémie (civil society group), 147

Habyarimana, Juvénal, 120, 123, 130, 153
happiness, 8, 9, 31–35, 37, 41, 59, 68, 80, 165, 182
Herod, 13, 105, 107, 165
hope, 2, 8, 9, 11, 12, 25, 34, 39, 41, 55, 61, 70, 75, 83–84, 85, 86–87, 88–89, 95, 98, 108, 124, 141, 142, 153, 162, 163–64
human rights, 11, 19, 60, 74, 121, 122, 147n2, 158n1, 161, 179, 183
Hutu, 17, 20–21, 25, 124, 126, 130, 136, 142, 143, 145, 149, 152, 153, 168–69, 173

ideology, 7, 10, 40, 41, 47, 51, 57, 59, 68–72, 122, 126, 167
Idjwi Island, 177
incarnation, 12, 19, 104–7, 110, 163–67
Interahamwe, 17, 21, 24, 126
ISTM (l'Institut Supérieur des Techniques Médicales de Bukavu), 171, 173
ITFM (l'Institut Technique Fundi Maendeleo), 96

Jesuit Province of Central Africa, 5
Jesuits. *See* Society of Jesus.
Jesus, 2, 8, 11, 12–13, 14, 18–20, 24, 33–34, 39, 41, 56, 83–84, 85–91, 93–94, 99, 100, 102, 103, 105–7, 109–10, 113, 118, 120, 124–25, 127, 129, 133, 138, 140, 160, 161–62, 165–67, 187
Job, 93, 113
John Paul II, Pope, 17, 97
John the Baptist, 124, 133, 138–39
justice, 2, 3, 7–8, 15, 25, 31, 53, 58–59, 60, 68, 71, 77, 80, 88–89, 90, 96–97, 109, 118, 119–20, 123, 125, 130, 133, 134, 136–37, 153, 179, 185
Justice et Paix France (commission), 142–43, 146–47
Justin Martyr, 183

Kabare monarchy, 5
Kabila, Laurent-Désiré, 23, 25
Kagame, Paul, 154
Kant, Immanuel, 58
Kasongo, 6
Kataliko, Emmanuel, 26
Katongole, Emmanuel, 2n1, 13n40

INDEX

Kibeho massacre, 20, 144, 147, 149, 152, 154
kingdom of God, 93, 105, 118, 119
Kivu region, 5, 22, 124, 135, 140, 143, 144, 148, 149, 151, 152, 154, 170, 177, 182, 183
    North, 22–23, 126, 177
    South, 4, 17, 22–23, 126, 156–57, 177
kleptocracy, 7, 65, 80
Kohn, Hans, 43
Kolbe, Maximilian, Saint, 166

Lenin, Vladimir, 51–52
Lent, 12, 92–94
liberation, 2, 8, 41, 61–62, 165
Liberia, 122, 182
love, 2, 3, 9, 13–14, 18–19, 22, 23–25, 33, 41, 42, 46, 54, 65, 68, 70, 73, 77, 89, 90, 91, 93–94, 97, 101–2, 103, 109, 110, 113, 124, 127, 129, 133, 140, 152, 166, 179, 186–87
Lukombo, 4
Luther, Martin, 44, 58

Machado, Antonio, 89
Malula, Joseph-Albert, Cardinal, 6, 7
Marshall Plan, 183
Martin of Tours, Saint, 141
martyr, 1, 13, 107, 110
Marx, Karl, 51, 59
Marxism, 51–52
Mary, 13–14, 24, 84, 85, 94, 107, 108, 110–11, 127, 134, 145, 165, 176, 181, 187
Maurice, Saint, 141
Misereor (German NGO), 135–37
Mobutu, Joseph-Désiré, 1, 2, 4, 6–12, 15, 18, 25, 145
Molla, Gianna Beretta, Saint, 101–2
Montesquieu, 68
Mora, Elisabetta Canori, Saint, 101–2
Moses, 104–5, 114
Mozambique, 122
Mudima, Admiral Muvua, 158–59
muhudumu ("watchman"), 14
Mukwege, Denis, 26–27

Mulamba, Colonel Léonard, 133, 140, 187
Mulele, Peter, 175n1
Mulungu refugee camp, 128
Munzihirwa, Christophe, life of
    activism during Rwandan refugee crisis 1, 3, 17–23
    archbishop of Bukavu, 1, 14, 17, 27, 100–103, 130–31
    assassination, 24
    beatification process, 27
    bishop of Kasongo, 5–6
    and Mobutu regime, 6–12, 15
    early life and education, 4–5
    Jesuit formation, 5
    Jesuit spirituality, 2, 3, 12–14, 16–17
    Jesuit Province of Central Africa, provincial of, 5
    legacy, 26–27
    ordination, 5
Museveni, Yoweri, 145

nation, 34–35, 37, 43–54, 97, 98, 125, 175, 182
nationalism, 1, 46, 51, 60
Nazi regime, 47, 120, 126
neocolonialism, 65, 131
Nero, 107
nonviolence, 12–13, 22, 85–91, 93–94, 109–10, 118, 124–25, 129, 139, 160, 163, 165–67, 179–87
Nuremberg Tribunal, 120
Nyere, Julius, 36–37

OZACAF (Office Zaïrois du Café), 165
Operation Turquoise, 126–27

palaver, 7, 66, 67, 75–80
Palestinian people, 136, 155
Panzi Hospital, 26, 172, 177
paschal mystery, 2, 12–13, 18–19, 25, 83–84, 85–91, 93–94
Pasinya, Laurent Monsengwo, Archbishop, 6
patience, 61, 67, 68, 76
Paul, Saint, 13, 86, 92, 107
Pax Christi (NGO), 142–43, 146n1, 147

INDEX

peace
  as tranquility of order, 16n57, 182
  and the family, 15–16, 89–90, 95–99
  in Great Lakes region, 3, 17–18, 21, 25–26, 102–3, 119–20, 125–27, 136–37, 142–43, 147, 148–50, 151–53, 155, 168–70, 172–74, 178–79
  of Christ, 85–89, 105, 119–20, 125, 129, 185
  in post-WWII Europe, 120, 183
  inner, 12, 25, 86, 88
  and education, 15–16, 98–99, 182–85
  and justice, 25, 88, 118, 119, 125, 136, 179
Péguy, Charles, 8, 70, 112
Pontius Pilate, 93, 94
proverbs, African, 5n7, 31–32, 37, 61, 62, 67, 69, 73, 76–77, 78, 85, 86, 95, 105, 124, 182
Prunier, Gérard, 20n78, 26

Rabelais, François, 184
RCD (Rassemblement Congolais pour la Démocratie), 26
reconciliation, 18, 25, 89, 120, 125, 127, 149, 150, 155, 167, 170, 173, 175, 179, 182–83, 185
refugees. *See* Rwandan refugee crisis.
religion, 3, 8, 11, 48, 55–61, 70–71, 92, 96
resurrection, 8, 11, 33, 39, 41, 62, 84, 85, 86, 107
revolution, 8–9, 13n40, 44, 50, 52, 56, 60, 68, 70, 71, 97
Robespierre, Maximilien, 71
Romero, Oscar, Saint, 3, 27
Rose-Croix, 57–58, 60
Rousseau, Jean-Jacques, 44
RPA (Rwandan Patriotic Army), 23–26, 150, 168–69, 172, 177
RPF (Rwandan Patriotic Front), 17, 21, 126, 128, 136, 147, 148–50, 151, 173, 178, 186
Rwanda, 20, 22–26, 126, 128, 130–31, 136, 142–45, 149–50, 152, 154–55, 159, 168–70, 172–73, 175–81, 186
Rwandan genocide (1994), 1, 3, 14, 17, 21, 126, 145, 149, 153
Rwandan refugee crisis, 17–25, 117–87
  attacks against refugees, 20, 22–23, 25–26, 144, 156, 177
  initial conditions, 17–18, 117–21, 128–30, 135–36
  deterioration in conditions, 20, 22–23, 142, 144, 146, 148–49, 161, 168, 172
  dismantling of camps, 23, 25–26
  hospitality for refugees, 3, 18–19, 22, 103, 118, 127, 129, 140, 144, 149, 152, 156, 159, 161, 173, 178, 183
  impact upon local population, 20, 129, 132, 135, 148–49, 151, 156–57, 158, 161, 164–65, 171–81, 183–84
  repatriation debate, 17–18, 21, 121, 136–37, 142–43, 149–55, 159, 161, 168–70, 172–74, 178–79
  role of Christian NGOs, 21, 135–37, 142–43, 146–47
  role of the Congolese Church, 18–20, 23–24, 124–25, 127, 152–53, 160, 161–62, 167, 171, 175–76, 180–81, 186–87
  role of the international community, 21, 121, 126–27, 128–29, 131, 136, 143, 148–50, 153, 168–70, 172–74, 183
  role of Rwandan government, 20, 22–26, 126, 128, 130–31, 136, 142–45, 149–50, 152, 154–55, 159, 168–70, 172–73, 175–81, 186
  role of UNHCR, 121, 128–29, 144, 152, 154–55, 159, 169
  role of Zairian government, 18, 21, 117–18, 129, 131, 132, 149, 151, 155, 156–59, 168, 173–74, 178, 180

SARM (Service d'Action et Renseignements Militaires), 158

Sauvy, Alfred, 39
Savimbi, Jonas, 122
Schramme, Jean, 103, 140, 180
Second Vatican Council, 90, 133, 139
secularity, 56–59, 70
Sieyès, Emmanuel Joseph, 44
silence, 16–17, 32, 112–14
simplicity, 16, 36
SNIP (Service Nationale d'Intelligence et de Protection), 165
Society of Jesus, 3, 5, 7
　Jesuit spirituality 2, 3, 12–14, 16–17
Socrates, 71
solidarity, 2, 9, 10, 18, 24, 41, 49, 52, 58–59, 69, 70, 72, 77, 79, 88, 96, 109, 110, 127, 153, 162, 175, 180
Solzhenitsyn, Aleksandr, 69, 71
Songasonga, Eugéne Kabanga, 6
Sovereign National Conference, 6, 75–80, 92, 96
Special Assembly for Africa of the Synod of Bishops (1994), 17, 100
spirituality, 2, 3, 4, 12–14, 16–17, 60, 83–84, 85–91, 112–14
Sudan, 122
suffering, 2, 12–13, 19, 25, 27, 83–84, 88, 93–94, 102, 113, 146, 161, 164
superstition, 60–61, 71

Tanzania, 36–37, 126
technology, 36, 38–40
Tertullian, 107
Tobit, 166
totalitarianism, 50, 52, 55, 66, 68–69, 71, 75, 122, 169
Touré, Sekou, 120
tradition
　African, 2, 5, 7–9, 32–33, 37, 39–40, 52–53, 55–57, 66, 75–80, 95, 98, 140 (*see also* proverbs, African)
　Christian, 2, 8–9, 11, 14, 19–20, 33–34, 38–39, 41–42, 55–61, 100–102, 109, 110, 124–25, 133, 139, 182
　See also enculturation
truth-telling, 4, 8, 10–11, 23, 59–60, 69, 73, 127, 153, 183, 186

Tutsi, 17, 21, 22, 24, 124, 126, 143, 145, 152, 153, 173, 178

Uganda, 37, 122, 145, 149, 178, 181
United Nations, 97, 131, 140, 151
　2010 report on violations of human rights in DRC, 25
　UN Secretary General, 1 (*see also* Boutros Boutros-Ghali)
　UNHCR (UN High Commissioner for Refugees), 119, 121, 128, 144, 152, 154–55, 159, 168, 169, 175
　UNAMIR (United Nations Assistance Mission for Rwanda), 126, 154
Universal Declaration of Human Rights, 74
United States of America, 48, 148, 169, 172–74

values, 11, 31, 35, 39, 40, 45, 46, 54, 70, 73–74, 77, 95–96, 109, 157, 175
violence, 6, 13, 19, 20, 22, 26, 52, 60, 69–70, 76, 88, 92–93, 97, 118, 122–27, 139, 143, 151, 154, 160, 171, 172, 177, 180
virtue, 15, 68, 71, 76, 97

Walungu, 4, 178
war, ethics of, 1–2, 18, 21–22, 25, 80, 120, 122–27, 132–34, 138–41, 147, 150, 154–55, 161–62, 173–74, 175–81, 183–84, 186–87
Wirtz, Karl, 135
wisdom, 33, 57, 59, 84, 97, 109, 184
WFP (World Food Program), 20, 144, 146, 155, 169
World War I, 47
World War II, 21, 25, 120, 125, 140n3, 183

Zaire. *See* Democratic Republic of the Congo.
Zaïre-Afrique (journal), 2, 4, 7–12, 14, 57
Zairian Civil Guard, 18, 117, 132, 158, 165, 173
Zairianization, 6

www.ingramcontent.com/pod-product-compliance
Lightning Source LLC
Chambersburg PA
CBHW021730220426
43662CB00008B/782